T0305283

Investing in
RUSSIA,
the UKRAINE,
LATVIA,
LITHUANIA and
KAZAKHSTAN

Investing in
RUSSIA,
the UKRAINE,
LATVIA,
LITHUANIA and
KAZAKHSTAN

GIL FEILER and
ALEXANDRE GARESE

sussex
ACADEMIC
PRESS
Brighton • Portland • Toronto

2 4 6 8 10 9 7 5 3 1

First published in 2007 in Great Britain by
SUSSEX ACADEMIC PRESS
PO Box 139
Eastbourne BN24 9BP

Distributed in North America by
SUSSEX ACADEMIC PRESS
ISBS Publisher Services
920 NE 58th Ave #300, Portland, OR 97213, USA

British Library Cataloguing in Publication Data
A CIP catalogue record for this book is available from the British Library.

Library of Congress Cataloging-in-Publication Data
Feiler, Gil.
   Investing in Russia, the Ukraine, Latvia, Lithuania and Kazakhstan / Gil Feiler and Alexandre Garese.
        p.   cm.
   Includes bibliographical references and index.
   ISBN 978-1-84519-243-3 (h/c : alk. paper)
    1. Investments, Foreign—Former Soviet republics.   2. Former Soviet republics— Economic conditions—1991–   I. Garese, Alexandre.   II. Title.

HG5572.F45   2007
330.947—dc22
                                                                       2007013588

Printed and bound by CPI Group (UK) Ltd, Croydon, CR0 4YY
This book is printed on acid-free paper.

Contents

List of Tables

Acknowledgements

This book was made possible by many people. Some helped the project along at every phase; others were the sine qua non for a particular challenge. The rest have advanced our broader effort to understand the business reality in the countries under discussion.

The authors would like to extend our sincere appreciation to the staff of Info-Prod Research Ltd. In particular, we would like to highlight the valuable contribution made by Ms. Tova Reznicek. She has worked tirelessly to promote and prepare this book. Her professionalism and critical eye are greatly acknowledged.

We would also like to express our gratitude to Anthony Grahame, Editorial Director at Sussex Academic Press, for his assistance in the publishing process.

Executive Summary

The economies of Central and Eastern Europe (CEE) and of the Commonwealth of Independent States (CIS) are currently undergoing a process of transformation that is expected to result in some of the most exciting investment opportunities currently available. The region is quickly becoming a powerful player on the world economic stage with the help of the growing interest and capital of international investors, vast human and natural resources, impressive economic reform and a growing trend by regional entrepreneurs to invest locally.

Although energy and commodities clearly represent the biggest commercial draw for investors in the foreseeable future, countless other opportunities, such as tourism, construction, and agricultural related projects, to name a few, have also proven lucrative for many investors.

Traditionally, the inability of the former Soviet governments and banking systems to finance large infrastructure projects deterred investments. However, local banks have begun to cooperate with western financial institutions, effectively pooling their capital to finance large scale projects. Furthermore, the region's various stock markets are also beginning to liberalize and open up to foreign investment. Foreign investors have witnessed greatly improved business prospects as a result of the implementation of essential economic reforms which focus on the private sector as the main source of investment and employment opportunities. Local authorities are also working to significantly lower tariff and non-tariff barriers to trade, while at the same time developing a skilled workforce to support sustainable private-sector growth. These facts represent significant business opportunities for both multinationals and small and medium enterprises.

In particular, the environment in the region is considerably more favorable to international investors. Western tastes are increasingly the norm in the region, with nearly 280 million potential consumers in the CIS alone. The proliferation of western franchises in recent years demonstrates just how hungry the region is for new, high-quality products. Meanwhile, local youth has demonstrated a greater affinity for international entertainment and consumer goods than did their parents' generation, whose tastes were often more locally oriented.

With ongoing privatization and liberalization, along with rising living standards pulling purchasing power along with it, foreign investors expect to see even further opportunities for investment in the near future. Multinationals with an interest in major projects are entering into the region, using projects based in single countries to establish relationships and build their reputations with local companies. Already established, as well as new companies are continuing to expand in order to take advantage of anticipated opportunities.

Many new infrastructure projects have been launched, improving the region's transportation, telecommunications, water, sewage, and energy systems, and setting the stage for further economic and social development. Progress has also been made in granting greater patent, trade mark and copyright protection and other intellectual property rights, largely as a result of international pressure.

It is clear that the prospects of lucrative returns on investments in the region far outweigh the challenges of investment within it. Such challenges include the slow pace of economic and political reform, as well as instability and minority extremism in some areas. Although political reform is not likely to come as quickly as economic reform, the lack of political freedom also helps ensure a relatively stable environment in which to invest.

The focus of this book is five nations, three of which are members of the CIS – Russia, Ukraine and Kazakhstan – along with the two Baltic states of Latvia and Lithuania. These countries exemplify the many opportunities as well as challenges for foreign investment in the region. The economies of each nation during the 1990s faced both political and economic upheaval following the collapse of the Soviet Union. With highly varied human and natural resources, strategic location and receptivity to market liberalization, each developed differently and at a different pace. Today, these countries represent five very different economic markets with equally differing opportunities for investment. Although the emergence of the institution of private property in each of them can be described as one of the most significant developments in modern history as in all former Soviet Republics, the question of how such a trend will proceed, especially in Russia, has surfaced. Russia's President Vladimir Putin has maintained that the nation's energy sector must serve the interests of the state, and that the fire-sale of some of these assets in the 1990s was a major blow to Russia's economic strength. The sale of Yukos' most valuable asset, Yugaskneftgaz, to state-controlled Rosneft along with the more recent sale of Sibneft to the state-dominated giant Gazprom, reflect the desire of the Kremlin to assert greater control over the commanding heights of the Russian economy. Nonetheless, Russia's energy sector continues to draw the attention of foreign investors hoping to reap the rewards the nation's vast natural energy resources, despite setbacks to privatization.

So too, has the energy sector of Ukraine won the attention of investors worldwide, while its quickly developing economy has spurred the interest of many entrepreneurs hoping to ride the wave of regional economic growth.

Kazakhstan, if only for its impressive size (five times that of of France), calls attention to itself as a potentially powerful regional player. Its rich natural energy reserves, along with vast human capital and impressive political and economic reforms, have translated into potential profit for both local investors and international ones alike.

Meanwhile, Latvia and Lithuania, which joined the European Union in May 2004, offer foreign investors impressive local growth rates as well as an exceptional stepping stone to larger economies such as Russia and other neighboring countries. Ascension to the EU for the two has significantly heightened the interests of foreign companies in further intensifying their activities in both countries. Indeed, foreign investments in Lithuania increased from around $5 billion in 2002 to more than $9 billion in 2006. At the time this book goes to print (July 2007), the Lithuanian economy is expected to continue to register high growth rates, while Latvia's economy will have registered the highest growth rate in the EU for 2006, a trend expected to continue into 2007.

A separate chapter is devoted to each of the five nations, and includes a survey of their respective political backgrounds, economic reviews, business and legal environments. In addition, leading investment-worthy sectors are highlighted, including pharmaceuticals, energy, IT and others, while a brief case study of a notable foreign business venture in each country is documented. Finally, each chapter concludes with a comprehensive list of internet resources which will prove indispensable for the prospective investor.

The information contained in this book was obtained from a broad spectrum of financial sources including: the International Monetary Fund and the World Bank, major accounting and consulting firms such as PriceWaterhouse Coopers and Ernst & Young, commercial services of several countries including the US, UK and Canada, official government sources of each of the five nations discussed, numerous recent academic texts as well as economic reports from international and local press sources. Unless otherwise noted, all data is up to date through February 2007.

Chapter 1

Investing in Russia

WITH ABUNDANT NATURAL RESOURCES, 140 million consumers, and impressive economic reform, conditions in Russia are ripe for long-term economic growth. The Russian economy has sustained continual growth in recent years as a result of an intensive economic reform program along with high oil prices worldwide. Additionally, Russian energy reserves, along with vast amounts of timber, steel, as well as palladium, platinum, diamonds, nickel, and gold (of which Russia is one of the world's largest producers) have boosted the Russian economy and continue to supply a large portion of the nation's federal budget revenues.

In particular, brisk exports of oil and natural gas, which doubled in 2006 to reach $90 billion, have helped Russia become the world's 10th largest economy in terms of gross domestic production in 2006, with its GDP standing at $975.3 billion and per capita GDP at $6,861. The achievement is notable considering the fact that just one year earlier, the nation's GDP stood at just $223.3 billion, and represented the world's 14th largest economy. With such growth sustained, forecasts predict that Russia will overtake Italy, France and Britain within two years to become the world's 6th largest economy. Meanwhile, Russia's hard currency reserves rose 66.7 percent to reach $303.7 billion, the third largest in the world. Additionally, the government's Stabilization Fund, which absorbs extra oil revenues and controls inflation, is close to $100 billion. It is therefore no surprise that a growing number of foreign investors have been attracted to the country despite the challenges of doing business there. More foreign banks have also begun to operate in Russia, resulting in more cash circulating within the economy. In early 2007, the Bank of Russia announced that Russia's foreign-exchange reserves reached $303.9 billion, making it the world's third largest foreign reserve owner after China and Japan. Despite the fact that Russians experience difficulties in acquiring adequate financial resources, consumer spending has nonetheless risen. A steady currency and an impressive construction boom in major urban areas are also signs of promising growth in the nation.

Growth in Russia's retail and consumer sector continues to be a significant driving force behind overall economic growth, propelled largely by the rapid growth in real disposable incomes in recent years. In 2006 total goods exports grew by an impressive 28 percent year on year in US dollar terms, and import growth accelerated to nearly 29 percent. The current-account surplus is forecast to peak for 2006 before slipping back slightly in 2007 and 2008. However oil-driven trade surpluses will more than offset deficits on the income and services accounts, with experts predicting that in 2007 Russia will become the world's largest oil exporter, ahead of Saudi Arabia. Meanwhile, the capitalization of the Russian stock market by the end of 2006 exceeded $1 trillion, while throughout the year the RTS index (the main indicator of Russia's stock market development) rose by 65 percent, representing some of the best results worldwide.

In all, Russia's financial reputation and investment climate have been improving significantly despite facing challenges. According to leading rating agencies Fitch and Standard & Poor's, Russia's sovereign-debt rating is only one step below grade A (high solvency). Moreover, Russia's growth rates in recent years make it the fastest growing economy in the western Hemisphere. With ample reserves protecting the country from unexpected external shock, coupled with economic reform programs and the authorities' fiscal policy, the nation's macroeconomic stability is ensured, along with solvency, the ability to guarantee the stability of its currency, and the continued interest of foreign investors.

POLITICAL BACKGROUND

POLITICAL STRUCTURE

After decades of social and economic stagnation in the Soviet Union, General Secretary Mikhail Gorbachev in 1985 introduced *glasnost* (openness) and *perestroika* (restructuring) into the region in an attempt to modernize the Communist regime. However, by 1991 the freedoms allowed the Soviet public under *glasnost* policies inadvertently led to their outspoken criticism of the regime. Calls for greater independence from Moscow's rule grew louder throughout the Soviet Union and in the Baltic Republics of Estonia, Lithuania and Latvia in particular. Discontent and the relaxation of media censorship enabled the Soviet public to voice its hitherto suppressed opinion, which led to the eventual disintegration of the Soviet Union into 15 independent republics. That same year, Boris Yeltsin won the first democratic presidential election, and was re-elected in July 1996.

The Russian Federation is governed by a two-chamber legislature consisting of the lower house, the State Duma, which has 450 deputies, and the upper house, the Federation Council, which has 178 deputies. Two Federation Council deputies are chosen from each of Russia's 89 republics and regions by regional governors and legislative bodies. In the 2007 election, all 450 seats in the Duma will be elected from party lists in a single nationwide constituency on a proportional basis. Universal direct suffrage is afforded to all Russian citizens over the age of 18. The President is elected for a four-year term, while the national government is appointed by the prime minister, who is appointed by the president.

During the 1990s, Russia's party political scene was extremely volatile and fragmented. However, it has since begun to settle. Today, Russia's political parties define themselves primarily by their support or opposition to the Kremlin rather than parties offering competing programs to distinct social groups, as is the case in western-style political systems.

KEY FIGURES

Russia's President Vladimir Putin was elected in 2000 and re-elected in 2004. Dmitry Medvedev serves as Russia's first deputy prime minister, while Sergei Naryshkin is Cabinet Chief of Staff.

Under Putin's leadership Russia has undergone some recentralization, as he consolidated and reinforced the power of the executive branch of government. He is expected to step down in 2008 after completing his second term in adherence with the constitutional ban on a third term in office. Significant power struggles in the Kremlin are expected to follow Putin's departure from office, since rival factions surrounding the president will likely put up strong fights for influence. Many factions, especially regional governors, are expected to seek to anticipate Putin's choice and position themselves accordingly.

Although the scenario is unlikely, speculation also continues over the possibility that Putin may attempt to remain in power following 2008, either in some official capacity or behind the scenes. However, there remains little risk of serious political instability as such turbulence will be temporary and contained. Moreover, as long as Russia continues to reap the rewards of its impressive oil and gas revenues, few of its citizens will express dissatisfaction with governmental authoritarianism.

Currently, some of the key parties in Russia's government are the United Russia Party, the Communist Party of the Russian Federation (CPRF), the Rodina (Motherland) Party, the Liberal Democratic Party of Russia (LDPR), and the Yabloko and Union of Rightist Forces (SPS) parties.

POLITICAL DEVELOPMENTS AND FOREIGN RELATIONS

Since the break-up of the Soviet Union, Russia has struggled to build a modern democratic political system with a market economy to replace the former controls in place during the Communist period. Much progress has since been made on several fronts. Today Russia is a key actor in the UN Security Council and an important partner of the EU, being its largest neighbor. The two bodies were brought even closer to the EU by the 2004 enlargement. Russia is also a member of the G-8, the Commonwealth of Independent States (CIS), Union of Russia and Belarus, Organization for Security and Cooperation in Europe (OSCE) and the North Atlantic Cooperation Council (NACC). It has played an important role in the mediation of international disputes including promoting peace in Kosovo and the Middle East. It has supported UN and multilateral initiatives in the Persian Gulf, Cambodia, Angola, the former Yugoslavia, and Haiti. Russia has also contributed troops to the NATO-led stabilization force in Bosnia.

The 2003 European Security Strategy situated Russia as a key player on geo-political and security issues at a global and regional level. In 2004, Russia and its other key neighboring force, China, divided up the islands in the Amur, Ussuri, and Argun Rivers, ending a century-old border dispute. A key dispute formally ending World War II hostilities between Russia and Japan continues over the sovereignty of the "Southern Kurils," as they are known in Russia, or the "Northern Territories," as they are known in Japan. Seabed treaties have been signed and ratified with Azerbaijan and Kazakhstan in the Caspian Sea though no consensus exists on dividing the water column among the littoral states. Some Finnish groups advocate restoration of Karelia, ceded to the Soviet Union following World War II along with other territories, though the Finnish Government has made no formal territorial demands. Russia and Norway dispute their maritime limits in the Barents Sea and Russia's fishing rights beyond Svalbard's territorial limits within the Svalbard Treaty zone. The Estonia – Russia technical border agreement was initialed in 1996 though both have been hesitant to sign and ratify it. A sometimes violent conflict continues to this day in Chechnya. Certain small but strategic segments as well as a maritime border remain contested by Russia and Georgia, and at the end of 2006, the latter accused Russia of espionage, after which it demanded that Russia vacate its military bases located on Georgian soil. That incident followed Russia's diplomatic and energy war on pro-western Georgian premier Mikhail Saakashvili, a move that did not hinder US approval of Russia's admission into the World Trade Organization.

Some analysts maintain that there is a strong interrelation between economic and political developments in post-Soviet Russia, and that economic crises have polarized and radicalized the Russian political arena. In addition, Russia's economy, they assert, is increasingly dependent on political developments.

ECONOMIC REVIEW

OVERVIEW

For most of the 1990s the Russian economy was in free fall, forcing most of its citizens to struggle merely to make ends meet. Since then, however, Russia's economy has demonstrated an impressive ability to overcome such challenges to become one of the fastest growing economies in the region.

Private domestic demand was boosted as a result of the growing income levels of the population. Russia's GDP growth in 2006 is estimated to have reached 6.5 percent year on year in the third quarter, up from 7.4 percent in the second, as strong domestic demand drove Russia's current economic expansion. Although such performance is reasonable in comparison to most economies, it is nonetheless below the pace of growth in much of the CIS as well as in other emerging markets such as China and India. Additionally, during the first six months of 2006, Russian economic growth slowed somewhat as compared with the corresponding period of the previous year as a result of a decrease in the first quarter of 2006 following weakening construction due to severe weather conditions. During the second quarter of 2006 the sector recovered with figures being stronger than projected and retail trade notably expanding. Also that year, Russian economic policy emphasis continued to alternate between attempting to fight inflation and prevent excessive real appreciation, which, in recent years has eroded the competitiveness gains from the 1998 devaluation. Today the Russian ruble (RUB) is valued at approximately .04 US dollars (1 US dollar equals approximately 26 RUB).

Similar though somewhat slower growth, however, is expected in 2007–8, though soaring oil prices are expected to underpin buoyant expansion of domestic demand and limit the extent of the output slowdown. Experts also forecast GDP growth of 5.9 percent in 2007 and 5.4 percent in 2008. This is due to capacity constraints acting as a brake on energy production. Booming domestic demand, on the other hand, will sustain an average annual pace of economic expansion of more than 5 percent. Inflation is expected to ease only moderately as a result of strong unsterilized foreign-exchange inflows. The

Table 1.1   Business Procedural Ranking

Ease of...	2006 rank	2005 rank	Change in rank
Doing business	96	97	+1
Starting a business	33	38	+5
Dealing with licenses	163	164	+1
Employing workers	87	88	+1
Registering property	44	40	-4
Getting credit	159	160	+1
Protecting investors	60	58	-2
Paying taxes	98	111	+13
Trading across borders	143	137	-6
Enforcing contracts	25	25	0
Closing a business	81	80	-1

Source: The World Bank, <www.doingbusiness.org/ExploreEconomies – Russia>.

Table 1.2   Key Indicators

	2005	2006	2007*
Real GDP growth	6.4	6.6	5.9
Consumer prices (% change)	12.7	9.7	9.1
Budget balance (% of GDP)	7.5	6.5	5.1
Merchandise exports (US$ bn)	243.6	310.1	344.5

Source: Economist Intelligence Unit, Country Risk Service, Russia.
*Forecast.

Table 1.3   Government Financial Data

Category	Latest Data* (November 2006)
Revenues	5,661.3
Tax revenues	5,168.1
Non-tax revenues	218.2
Expenditure	5,320.4
Interest expenditure	157.3
Non-interest expenditure	5,163.1
Balance, deficit/surplus	-340.9
Financing (net)	-340.09
Domestic	-1,112.3
Bank	-1,228.4
Non-bank	116.1
Foreign	771.4

Source: Russian Ministry of Finance, <http://www1.minfin.ru/sdds/nsdp.htm>.
*RUB billion.

current-account surplus will narrow somewhat, though it is projected to reach around US $75 billion, or 5.7 percent of GDP in 2008.

Few advances in structural reform are likely in the run-up to the 2007–8 elections, as relatively prudent macroeconomic policies will be maintained. Russia's economic policy will likely focus on raising the standards of living though "national priority projects." Such projects increase public spending on health, education and housing, and on increasing the birth rate. In addition, the government is expected to continue and expand its policy of establishing state control over the "commanding heights of the economy," as is currently the case in Russia's energy and metals resources. Preliminary figures for 2006 show that the current-account surplus of the Central Bank rose to $80 billion, up from some $62 billion during the same period of 2005. Russia's institutional and policy forecast are mixed. On one hand, political and macroeconomic stabilization which has occurred in recent years has signifi-

Table 1.4   Government Indicators (percentage of GDP)

	2005	2006	2007*
Overall balance	8.1	7.6	4.7
Revenue	40.0	39.8	37.9
Expenditures	31.9	32.3	33.2
Primary balance	9.2	8.4	5.2
Non-oil balance	−5.9	−7.4	−8.3
Federal govt. balance	7.5	6.9	4.0

Source: International Monetary Fund Public Information Notice PIN No. 06/128.
*Forecast.

cantly improved the business environment. On the other hand, the overall business environment remains unpredictable, and the concentration of economic power in the hands of a few massive conglomerates hampers competition. Ongoing attempts to reverse such conditions are expected, though inefficiency and a cumbersome bureaucracy will likely stand in the way of such measures.

ENERGY

Oil and gas sales now make up two-thirds of total export receipts in Russia. As a result of high oil prices, Russia's export value also rose. Meanwhile, the inflow of foreign investment swelled by 40 percent year on year. Of this amount, 70 percent consisted of borrowing from residents abroad.

Russia's No. 1 firm, Gazprom, holds approximately 25 percent of the world's natural-gas reserves. Assembled from assets of the former Soviet Gas Ministry and largely privatized in the 1990s, the Russian government increased its former minority stake to a controlling 51 percent in 2005. Today Gazprom has a market capitalization of around $250 billion, putting it in the class of international firms such as Exxon and General Electric. For over a year

Table 1.5   External Sector Indicators (annual percentage change)

	2005	2006	2007*
Export volumes	4.8	4.7	4.7
Oil	2.7	3.4	3.7
Gas	3.4	2.0	2.0
Non-energy	8.0	7.0	6.7

Source: International Monetary Fund Public Information Notice PIN No. 06/128.
*Forecast.

now, however, the energy giant has been accused of openly using natural gas for geopolitical purposes and as a tool of the Kremlin by charging market rates for its gas to importers from the CIS. At the beginning of 2006, Gazprom halted gas supplies to Ukraine after it balked at seeing their gas prices rise from $65 to $230 per 1,000 cubic meters. The move triggered gas deficits in a freezing Europe, most of whose gas is transported through Ukraine from Russia. During the course of the year there were other similar incidents involving Russia and former Soviet republics. One such incident was justified in the Russian media as being in response to Kremlin-unfriendly Ukrainian president Viktor Yushchenko. The end of 2006 saw yet another gas war with Belarus, which risked disruption of supplies to western Europe and damaging Russia's relations with the West further.

Gazprom continues to strengthen its positions in Turkmenistan, from which it receives fairly high discounts in gas, as well as Uzbekistan, and Kazakhstan, in which it is increasing gas production. Through 2008, the difference between the volume of gas produced by the company and that used in domestic and foreign markets will be also expanded with imports from former Soviet republics. The most likely supplier, of course, is Turkmenistan, which already has a gas pipeline network. Also in an attempt to increase Russia's presence abroad and keep domestic energy resources under state control, Lukoil, with a market capitalization of around $80 billion, began investing in South America, the Middle East and North Africa, and purchased a refinery in Bulgaria. Another Russian oil giant, Rosneft, with a market capitalization of some $100 billion, has also expressed interest in expanding its refining capacities outside of Russia. The country has already revealed plans to double its exports of oil to China and is in partnership with CNOOC, China's largest oil company, to build an oil refinery and run gas stations in China.

Presence in Poland is also impressive, with Gazprom being the fifth largest foreign company in Poland, according to Liuhto & Jumpponen (2002). Gazprom also has equity investments at least in two Polish companies, including Gas Trading and Europol Gaz. Gazprom's success is expected to continue. It currently is the world's second-largest energy company after Exxon-Mobil. Its net profits rose from $490 million in 2001 to $11.7 billion in 2005, and 80 percent in 2006, exceeding industry giants Shell and BP last year. It is currently valued at about $262 billion.

In the coming years it is expected that Russia will use the power of Gazprom and its vast oil and gas resources to trigger shifts in power equations, a trend that was begun by Putin when he began to reinstate government control over Russia's energy assets that had been privatized under former President Boris Yeltsin. The trend was especially threatening to western energy giants, when in 2006 they suffered two major setbacks in their attempts to win a foothold in the Russian energy market: the first setback occurred in October when Gazprom changed it plans to give a 49 percent interest to western firms in the Shtokman field in the Barents Sea and decided to retain full ownership of the world's biggest gas reserve holding 3.7 trillion cubic meters of natural gas; and the second in December, when Gazprom ousted Royal Dutch Shell from its leading position in Asia's biggest energy project, Sakhalin-2. Some experts believe that the moves and future plans to further erode western control over Russia's energy sector could effectively erode the West's post-Cold War gains. Others believe that tightened state control could translate to profits for foreign investors who wish to invest in the industry without insisting on controlling rights. Up to 49 percent of Rosneft may soon be sold to outside investors to repay $7.5 billion the state borrowed to acquire a majority stake in Gazprom. Others believe that restrictions on Gazprom purchases by foreigners may also be lifted. Recent industry reports reveal that the US Chevron Corp. of San Ramon, as well as Italian energy companies Eni SpA and Enel SpA, are interested in buying disputed assets of OAO Yukos, whose largest production unit was bought some years back by OAO Rosneft after an opaque auction. Though it is unlikely that such a strategic asset would be sold to a foreign company, the current declarations of interest in participating in the liquidation of a business that in previous years drew protests from abroad and shook investor confidence in Russia, underscores the weight of the Russian oil sector.

BUSINESS ENVIRONMENT

OVERVIEW

As a result of Russia's vast pool of natural resources, most major corporations operating in Russia have concluded that presence in Russia is essential to the success of business ventures in the country. However, the nation's economy suffers from an over-reliance on raw materials. Between 2000 and 2005, unprocessed raw materials accounted for a rising share of exports, increasing from 80 percent to 85 percent.

President Putin has repeatedly emphasized the importance of foreign investment as a critical element of Russia's economic development. Nonetheless, in some cases Russian authorities have been less willing to permit investment strategies that keep project control in foreign hands. While in practice the government has favored joint ventures with local entities or direct cash investments, Russia's commitment to foreign investment has been unclear, especially when concerning the energy sector.

The Kremlin's recent determination to establish control over Russia's energy sector will result in unfavorable production-sharing agreements from the 1990s to be revised, while foreign investors will be limited to minority stakes. Policy trends such as forcing Shell (UK) to cede control of Sakhalin-2 to Gazprom are likely to lead to similar moves against BP (UK) and Total (France).

Other major barriers to investment in Russia's market remain the somewhat erratic transition from a socialist, centrally planned economy to a more open, market-oriented one. In addition, significant government bureaucracy and weak rule of law affect the market significantly in areas such as business establishment, tax collection, dispute settlement, property rights, product certification and standards, as well as Customs clearance. Meanwhile, finding qualified local partners and employees, especially those that understand western business norms and speak proficient English, can be extremely challenging. At times, it can be unclear to foreign investors which sectors are open to them for investment without Russian majority partners. Russian consumers are generally price sensitive, but are oftentimes willing to pay for quality, especially for a recognized brand.

Several sources of project financing in Russia are available, including: The World Bank International Finance Corporation for areas of agribusiness, oil and gas, mining, power, telecommunications, IT, financial services, manufacturing, services and infrastructure; the European Bank for Reconstruction and Development for investment in infrastructure and financial services, and the Black Sea Trade and Development Bank (BSTDB) for investment in telecommunications, manufacturing, financial services, transportation, energy, agribusiness and tourism. In addition, two specialist banks which provide export financing are the Moscow Narodny Bank and the Trade Finance Team at HypoVereinsbank.

PRIVATIZATION

Approximately three-quarters of the Russian economy has been privatized, though many privatized enterprises continue to have significant state-held blocks of shares. Recently, however, major steps on the part of the Kremlin have turned back the clock in terms of Russian privatization reforms; for example, in 2006 Russia's aircraft producers were deprivatized and merged into a single state-run conglomerate. Another major deprivatization move took place when the Russian state arms monopoly Rosoboronexport took over AVISMA, the world's largest titanium producer, which supplies to Airbus and Boeing. Along with significant expansion of state-control over the nation's energy sector, such as a recent law giving Gazprom the sole right to export Russian gas, some economists and political commentators maintain that diamonds, forestry, telecommunications, automobiles, and banking will also face similar restructuring.

Some privatization of remaining state holdings is scheduled to continue, and some of these offerings may be considered good buys by some investors. Foreign investors are advised to work closely with appropriate local, regional and federal officials that exercise ownership and other authority over companies whose shares they may want to acquire. The slow pace of structural reforms and the increasing role of the state in the energy sector are most probably the main causes for the continued disappointing results for foreign investment.

BANKING

While the Russian banking system remains relatively small, it is one of the fastest-growing sectors of the economy today as a result of macroeconomic stability, a high rate of economic growth, a surge in investments, and increased consolidation. Additionally, a credit boom, the rehabilitation of bank payment settlement systems, an increase in income and savings, and the growth of demand for investment resources have been key factors in continued growth. Furthermore, the Central Bank of Russia has achieved visible results in banking sector reform, which is being carried out in order to increase sustainability, functionality, transparency and reliability of the banking system. Russian banks are also playing a more effective and normal role in the economy by collecting savings from more and more depositors and distributing them through loans and other types of financing to more productive uses.

Despite such progress, the sector remains one of the weakest areas in Russia's reform program, and has yet to efficiently perform its basic role of financial intermediary. Nevertheless, it continues to evolve in terms of being able to meet the capital and credit needs of a rapidly growing and dynamic market economy. Today, it is estimated that approximately one-third of the population still prefers to keep their personal savings to themselves rather than trust their savings to banks.

While data indicates that some 40 percent of Russia's banks are wholly foreign-owned, the government has attempted to enhance the stability and efficiency of the sector. The Central Bank of Russia thus adopted the Banking Sector Development Strategy to increase the protection offered to depositors and creditors; to enhance the banking sector's role as a primary intermediary for household and commercial credit operations; to improve the Russian banking sector's competitiveness; to protect the financial sector from illicit activity such as money laundering and the financing of terrorism; to improve transparency in the sector; and to build investor, creditor, and depositor confidence.

In 2005, the Central Bank of Russia completed its review of all banks that sought admission to the recently established Deposit Insurance System (DIS). To gain admission to the DIS, a bank had to verifiably demonstrate to the Central Bank that it complies with Russian identification and transparency requirements. Currently, 927 of Russia's estimated 1200 banks have been admitted to the DIS, effectively weeding out over 200 banks from Russia's banking system. The most active foreign banks in Russia are Citibank, Raiffeisenbank Austria, ING Eurasia Bank and ABN Amro, along with the European Bank of Reconstruction and Development (EBRD), which deals primarily in project financing.

In 2007–8, the Central Bank is expected to seek to prevent significant ruble strengthening and continue large-scale foreign-exchange inflows. Continued real appreciation, albeit at a slower rate, is also expected.

However, a company doing business in Russia can easily access an expanding range of basic banking services offered by the larger commercial banks. In the case of foreign investors, only authorized banks are permitted to open special bank accounts for resident individuals ("F" Accounts), and resident entrepreneurs and legal entities ("R1" and "R2" accounts). Non-residents in Russia can open the following special accounts: "S" accounts to trade sovereign ruble bonds, "A" accounts to trade shares in unit investment funds, "O" accounts to trade non-sovereign ruble bonds, "V1" accounts to receive ruble loans from residents, and "V2" accounts to give loans to residents as well as to buy certain types of securities from residents.

Today, the rate of increase in the volume of loans provided by Russian banks exceeds GDP growth. Several western investment banks and venture funds have increased the size of their project finance portfolios, while a number of bilateral and multilateral financial institutions continue to facilitate trade and investment in both the public infrastructure and private sectors. The use of long-term, limited recourse project financing, however, remains limited by such factors as the immaturity of commercial legislation, poor contract enforcement, a lack of transparency in beneficial ownership, the inefficient process and high cost of collateralizing project assets, limited rights of debt and equity holders, and weak contractor performance requirements.

CURRENCY

A series of amendments were made to Russian law on currency controls in recent years. Generally, companies and individuals face no significant difficulty in obtaining foreign exchange though the ruble (RUB) is the only currency that is legal tender in Russia. The Central Bank in Russia put a number of regulations into effect designed to implement amendments to

Federal Law No. 173-FZ "On Currency Regulation and Currency Control." Foreign currency transactions between residents and non-residents involving non-cash settlements must be carried out using special bank accounts.

Only authorized banks can carry out the sale or purchase of foreign currency transactions. According to currency control laws, the Central Bank retains the right to impose restrictions on the purchase of foreign currency.

Controls on current transactions proceeds from the sale of exported goods for foreign currency must be credited back to the exporter's account in an authorized bank.

The Government of Russia has implemented a wide range of major economic reforms, including the gradual removal of currency control restrictions. The Central Bank of Russia is now responsible for currency operations related to loans and financing, securities transactions and banking operations. The Central Bank is likely to pursue a flexible exchange-rate policy in order to meet the government's year-end inflation target. However, money supply growth, generally running at more than 40 percent will likely result in a small overshoot of its expected target.

Meanwhile, the government of Russia regulates currency operations relating to foreign trade, such as the export and import of goods, works and services, intellectual property and participation of residents in the charter capital of foreign companies other than joint-stock companies.

Among the most important new principles introduced by recent laws on currency are the provision of an exhaustive list of currency operations subject to administrative regulation and the establishment of a "free hands" regime with respect to other currency operations between residents and non-residents by introducing the presumption that such currency operations should be free of restriction. Foreign-exchange inflows and domestic demand growth are expected to remain strong in 2007–8, while inflation is likely to decline modestly.

TAXATION AND CUSTOMS

Russia's current tax legislation increasingly matches the needs of its growing market economy. However, as a result of major changes made to the nation's tax code in order to meet such needs, significant confusion is faced by those less familiar with the system. Consulting with a local tax expert, therefore, is highly advisable.

Value Added Tax (VAT) and Import Duties are collected on a basis similar to the EU model and calculated on the sales value. VAT is applied at a general uniform rate of 18 percent, with the exception of certain foodstuffs, pharmaceuticals and children's clothes, to which a lower rate of taxation is generally applied. Meanwhile, certain supplies are entirely exempt from VAT, such as particular financial services and medical equipment. Imports are subject to VAT and are calculated based on the customs value of the item plus customs duties and customs fees. In general, goods manufactured or assembled in Russia, whether by a Russian or foreign company, and then exported, are not subject to VAT. If these goods are exported before payment is received, then no VAT is collected. On the other hand, if payment is received before shipment, the exporter must pay the applicable VAT and then request a refund from the tax authorities. Enterprises that have advertising activity must pay a local tax, levied on the cost of advertising goods and services, excluding VAT. Advertising expenses are currently tax deductible.

A Customs Code which complies with WTO requirements recently went into effect. The new code reduces the role of the state and does not allow the Russian government or its agencies, including the Federal Customs Service (FCS), to create contradicting regulations and instructions. The new code reduces the length of time required for customs clearance significantly, and offers the possibility for advance declaration of cargo before its arrival at customs. The code also restricts the Russian Federation State Customs Committee from issuing contradictory additional regulatory acts, makes possible the settlement of disputes with customs authorities directly in a court of law, establishes a definitive and comprehensive list of documents that must be submitted for customs clearance, and prohibits the customs authorities from refusing to accept a declaration that contains inaccurate information. Despite the improvements, many amendments remain to be made to the code, since the most liberal and progressive provisions of the Customs Code have proved to be difficult to apply.

The customs value in Russia is generally considered to be the CIF (cost-insurance-freight) price of the goods imported, though a customs-processing fee also exists. Often, customs officials request the Shippers Export Declaration (SED), considered to be a sufficient proof of the customs value, though presenting SED is not mandatory and the importer can present other available documents. Import duties ranging from 0 percent to 30 percent of the CIF value of the goods being imported are imposed. Some goods are subject to specific duties defined as a certain amount per unit of weight. Duties are paid in rubles based on the current exchange rate. Customs clearance can take no longer than three days, though this period can be extended under certain circumstances.

Regarding land taxes, a tax may be levied on land according to its type and location. Areas such as St. Petersburg and Moscow generally have higher land tax rates than in rural areas. 'Profits tax' is levied on an enterprise's gross profits, for which a list of deductible expenses exists. Foreign companies operating in Russia are therefore able to benefit from the exemptions in Russia's dual taxation treaties.

Foreign legal entities without a business presence in Russia are subject to a withholding tax on freight services rendered in Russia, while dividends and interest are also taxed. Although personal income tax in Russia is a flat rate, there may be some withholding requirements for expatriates.

FREE SPECIAL ECONOMIC ZONES

Several free customs zones and warehouses exist in Russia in an attempt to encourage investment in specific areas. In 2005, six regions were awarded the right to establish Special Economic Zones (SEZ). These included the residential neighborhood of Moscow, Zelenograd (for microelectronics), Dubna, located in the Moscow Region (nuclear physics), St. Petersburg (information technologies and instrument making), and Tomsk (new materials). Industrial SEZs will also be established in the Lipetsk Region (household equipment and possibly furniture) and in Yelabuga located in the Republic of Tatarstan (aircraft components and chemical goods). The Kaliningrad Special Economic Zone (SEZ) has been able to attract some moderate investments as it provides advantages to foreign exporters and investors, as almost all goods imported into it are exempt from import customs duties, as long as they are not re-exported to the rest of Russia. Such products are also exempt from import duties and quotas when they are processed there with value added of at least 30 percent. An SEZ in Magadan has attracted minor amounts of investment and the SEZ in Nakhodka has reportedly never been implemented.

Enterprises operating in industrial-production zones (20 square kilometers) pay lower unified social taxes (with the highest rate reduced from 26 percent to 24 percent) and those within progressive-technical zones (2 square kilometers) are allowed to write-off all R&D expenses. Both types of zones benefit from reduced land and property taxes and a waiver of customs duties on imports and finished exports. The tender process will continue with more SEZs to be designated in the future.

Many larger foreign investors see little advantage to establishing businesses within one of the proposed SEZs, as investment incentives offered by local administrations are often more attractive than the SEZ benefits.

LABOR AND WAGES

Wage and employment deferentials in Russia's labor market can be vast, as the market remains fragmented, characterized by limited labor mobility across regions, and consequent wage and employment differentials. Unemployment across Russia in 2005, according to International Labor Organization (ILO) standards, ranges from approximately 7.6 percent to more than 40 percent. Unemployment in areas such as Moscow is about one percent, while average monthly incomes are approximately three times higher than the national average, or about $290 per month. Labor mobility is very restricted by an under-developed housing and mortgage market, and the continued existence of residency permits and registration. Subsidized housing and cultural and family connections often make workers reluctant to move, as well as lack of information about employment or housing opportunities in other parts of Russia. Such lack of labor mobility across regions significantly affects wage rates and employment. However, the labor force is generally well educated, though skilled labor has been in increasingly short supply.

Enterprises that pay wages in full and on time generally have smooth labor – management relations. However, worker safety is a major unresolved issue, as enterprises are often unable or unwilling to invest in safer equipment or to enforce safety. Laborers have increasingly pursued their demands through the court system or used methods such as rallies and days of action to call attention to their plight, relying less on strikes than during the mid-1990s, while the trade union movement is still largely dominated by the Federation of Independent Trade Unions of Russia (FNPR). Meanwhile, many new free trade unions outside this confederation have begun to make significant strides in defending their members' interests. The Russian government generally adheres on paper to International Labor Organization (ILO) conventions protecting worker rights, though enforcement is often lacking. A new Labor Code has been implemented seeking to diminish the role of government in setting and enforcing labor standards and to move toward more flexible labor markets.

A business is liable for the entire Unified Social Tax (UST), which

Table 1.6   Real Sector Data (December 2006)

Category	Unit	Latest Data
Economically active population	Million people (estimate)	74.3
Employed	Million people	69.1
Unemployed	Million people (estimate)	5.1
Officially registered unemployed	Million people	1.7
Consumer price index	2,000=100	224.8
Producer price index	2,000=100	257.4

Source: Russian Ministry of Finance, <http://www1.minfin.ru/sdds/nsdp.htm>.

replaced three separate funds paid into by employees. Under the updated law, no amount is actually withheld from employees, and the total liability for each employee is calculated on the basis of monthly gross pay. In accordance with the current Tax Code, the employer is obliged to pay UST for foreign individuals. Personal income tax is a flat rate.

FOREIGN DIRECT INVESTMENT

Foreign Direct Investment into Russia has been increasing at impressive rates in recent years as a result of laws and programs adopted in many regions in Russia to attract investment. Recent statistics published by the United Nations Conference on Trade and Development (UNCTAD) reveal that net outflow of capital in the amounts of $15, $20 or $25 billion in recent years were followed by massive inflow of private investment in Russia in 2006, including an unprecedented $41 billion, consisted of $28.4 billion of FDI, nearly double that of the previous year when the figure stood at $14.6 billion. More than $1 billion worth of Russian weapons is bought annually by China alone, making it Russia's biggest customer, with trade growing by nearly 40 percent in 2005. The impressive numbers make Russia the largest FDI recipient of all CIS and southeast European states.

Although tax reforms at the federal level aim to create a level playing field for all investors and limit the scope of incentives regions can offer, in practice large foreign investors continue to receive such incentives (although a completed investment project is often later expected to provide social services and other benefits to the local population). Chronic shortcomings in the investment climate continue to dampen the potential to attract FDI. The lack of clarity in Russian tax law and administration, inconsistent government regulation, unreliability of the legal system, and crime and corruption all dissuade such investment.

The 1991 investment code guarantees foreign investors rights equal to those of Russian investors (although some industries do have limits on foreign ownership – see below). The July 1999 law on foreign investment confirmed the principle of national treatment. This 1999 law includes a grandfather clause that protects certain large investments (over approximately $33 million) from unfavorable changes in tax or other legislation until the project's breakeven point, but for a period of not more than seven years. However, in practice, these protections have not been provided due to the lack of implementing regulations. The Russian government is developing other legislation to oversee, and possibly limit, foreign investment in "strategic sectors." What exactly constitutes a strategic sector is still undefined. However, it seems clear that the defense industry and national security sectors will fall into this category. While explicit restrictions on foreign direct investment have already been in effect for certain sectors, a 1998 law on the aerospace industry limits foreign ownership to 25 percent of an enterprise, though some existing joint ventures were "grandfathered," and in late 2005 legislation was passed eliminating foreign ownership limits in the natural gas monopoly Gazprom. For now, government experts are still locked in debate about whether to review individual investment deals on a case-by-case basis or to set across-the-board limits to foreign ownership in key sectors. Both positions have high-level backing and it remains unclear which approach will ultimately prevail.

In 2003, Russia enacted several amendments to the insurance law that effectively liberalized the market, allowing majority-owned Russian subsidiaries of insurers from the EU to sell life and mandatory forms of insurance in Russia. Although the law only permits those companies with offices in the EU to open subsidiaries which offer such types of insurance (life insurance and mandatory forms of insurance), the regulator has interpreted the legislation as allowing any foreign insurer to set up life insurance operations in Russia provided that the company has an office in the EU via which the investment is made. Russian law does not permit foreign insurance companies to establish branch offices in Russia.

Foreign direct investment (FDI) outflow from Russia has multiplied since the mid-1990s with the amount of FDI in 2000 being nearly ten-fold the mid-1990s amount. This would suggest that the financial position of certain Russian firms has improved significantly and led them to seek investment opportunities abroad, a trend that is expected to continue in the future. Russian multinationals have been investing heavily in emerging markets such as Belarus, Ukraine, Kazakhstan, Uzbekistan, and Africa, as well as in the West in places such as the United States. More than $200 million in Russian FDI has reached Bulgaria, with most of these investments being in the gas and oil industry. Russia's Lukoil has bought an oil refinery in Bulgaria. According to Liuhto & Jumpponen (2002), more than $130 million has been invested in Latvia by Russian firms, with the three biggest investments being Latrostrans, Latvijas Gaze and Lukoil Baltija. These three investments at the time accounted for more than 70 percent of the Russian FDI in Latvia. Lukoil is also the biggest Russian investor in Lithuania, with some $25 million invested in 2002 through Euro Oil Invest. In the US, a Russian company purchased the US Oregon Steel Mills for some $2.3 billion, while America's Rouge Industries, the fifth largest American steel producer and Ford supplier, was also bought by a Russian multinational firm.

MARKETING GOODS AND SERVICES

JOINT VENTURES

Many foreign firms enter into strategic partnerships with Russian firms by taking an equity position in Russian joint stock companies and establishing joint ventures (JV). Due to the potential risks, such ventures require extensive planning and sustained commitment. It is advisable in many cases to maintain managerial control while offering foreign partners minority stakes. Experience has shown that foreign minority shareholders face substantial difficulty in protecting their interests in Russian courts. In addition, while foreign companies may view a JV as an opportunity to secure a local partner in the Russian market, many Russian partners may see the foreign partner primarily as a source of capital and subsequently place little priority on local market development.

In all cases of joint ventures, large or small, it is crucial to establish a mutually beneficial partnership in which trust is established with Russian counterparts. Long-term commitments have also proven to have far more chances of success than short-term ones, as building trust can be a delicate matter requiring extensive input on the part of a foreign investor. Personal relations outside of the work environment are key to such trust in a way which is often underestimated by investors from the West.

Indeed, some findings suggest that a great number of Russians have become disenchanted with the experience of doing business with foreigners, a sentiment shared by foreign investors regarding their Russian counterparts as well. However, such ventures still hold many advantages for both parties, as exemplified by a large number of successful JVs in the country's business arena. Despite the risks, a JV can have many advantages since it allows a foreign entity to gain a measure of Russian identity – a helpful advantage in a culture which still views outsiders with some suspicion. A growing number of multinational enterprises (MNEs), as well as Asea Brown Boveri, General Motors, Budweiser, Heineken, Anheuser-Busch and countless smaller establishments have chosen to establish joint ventures in Russia.

FRANCHISING

Over the past decade, Russia's franchising sector has developed significantly, especially in areas such as fast food establishments, restaurants, retail, education and training, fitness and health-care, recreation and entertainment, travel and lodging, and automotive. Meanwhile, franchising in business-oriented services is growing in areas such as cleaning services and maintenance, transportation, logistics, express mail services, management training and

Table 1.7   Case Study – Nestlé Russia

Company: Nestlé Russia
Date established: 1995.
2006 Turnover: $1.3 billion.
Local market hold: has a controlling stake in domestic ice cream producer JSC Khladoprodukt.
Number of plants in Russia: Twelve dairy plants, five which supply 80 percent of the total volume of milk.

Company developments:
2002 – Nestlé acquires the Saint Springs in Russia based in Kostroma, 350 kilometres northeast of Moscow.

2004 – Nestlé begins construction of the Krasnodar Territory processing plant, employing 300 staff members.

2004–6 – Nestlé's share on Russia's mineral water market: down from 9.6 percent to 8.3 percent from 2004 to 2006. Nestlé's share on Russia's packaged chocolates: down from 24.4 percent to 12.7 percent in the same period.

Total Nestlé sales in Russia rose 19 percent during the first half of 2006. Nestle hopes to drive its holdings in its Russian factories to 100 percent.

2007 – In response to dwindling sales, Nestlé will reportedly form a partnership with local Russian group Bistroff to produce and distribute its range of hot cereals and porridge products.

Source: Nestle Russia, <www.nestle.ru>, local press reports.

consulting. Over the next few years expansion is expected in casual dining, as well as coffee shops and tea rooms. Opportunities also exist in the retail sector. In no area is the market saturated in terms of franchises.

MARKETING STRATEGIES

Telemarketing and fax marketing to business customers is fairly popular in Russia, though it is not particularly effective. Person-to-person direct marketing, on the other hand, has been found to be far more effective as well as cost effective. Some accounts indicate that direct sales accounted for nearly one-fifth of total cosmetics and toiletry sales in recent years.

   Foreign firms may participate in public tenders if the product or service is not available from domestic producers, or if Russian production is not considered economical, thus making regional or local authorities good potential customers for foreign suppliers.

As the number of internet users increases throughout Russia, so too does B2B e-commerce, especially in Moscow and St. Petersburg. However, lack of on-line payment mechanisms leaves such systems somewhat constrained. The Russian government's "E-Russia" program aims at stimulating the growth of e-commerce throughout the country using federal and local e-government initiatives as a catalyst.

ESTABLISHING A BUSINESS

Prior to establishing a business in Russia, it is essential to perform detailed market research to identify specific sector opportunities, and due diligence is extremely important. As a result of the immense size of Russia, most businesses therefore tend to approach the Russian market on a regional basis, with Moscow and St. Petersburg considered two of the best starting points.

Russian law offers several commonly used structures to conduct business, including a Limited Liability Company, a privately held, closed joint stock company, a publicly held, open joint stock company, a representative or branch office of a foreign company, or registration as an individual private entrepreneur.

Both foreign and domestic legal entities may establish, purchase and dispose of businesses in Russia. Investment in some sectors may be limited, such as those affecting national security (insurance, banking, natural resources, communication, transportation, and defense-related industries).

PROMOTION AND ADVERTISING

There are many ways to reach Russian customers, especially through Russia's vigorous print media. Television, radio, and billboard media are also common throughout Russia and are therefore relatively efficient means of promotion and advertising, while many international advertising agencies are active in Russia. Many publications exist which cater to specific interests, and are therefore good marketing tools. For consumer goods, traditional advertising media are well established including television, print media, billboards, magazines, displays, and free samples.

Russian trade shows are also an excellent way for a company to enter the Russian market, facilitating contact with potential buyers and distributors. Furthermore, representatives of regional governments and state enterprises from remote areas often visit exhibitions in major cities to purchase goods.

It is important to remember that foreign products have often faced tough competition against Russian products in the eyes of Russian citizens, therefore requiring the need to "Russify" advertising to suit Russian culture.

CHOOSING A DISTRIBUTION CHANNEL

There are four major ways of choosing a distribution channel for starting a business in Russia. These include: selecting an agent, using local distributors, opening a representation office and registering a foreign company in Russia (the latter being considered the most advanced means of operating a business in the country). Good personal relationships with representatives are extremely important.

Although there are several examples of major joint ventures with foreign investors which were forced to dissolve for failure to reach common ground with Russian partners or authorities, including the US General Motors, others remain as testament to the many success stories in the country. One example is London-based Daigeo plc, the world's largest liquor maker, and Moscow-based Alfa Group Consortium, owner of Smirnov, who teamed up to win anti-trust approval. Diageo is to pay $50 million to Alfa for a majority stake in Smirnov, and will then distribute the vodka and its own brands through a joint venture-ship with an Alfa subsidiary A1 Group. Another example is the recent decision by America's Budweiser to team up with Heineken Russia and Anheuser-Busch Companies. Through Heineken, the brand will be distributed via its network in Russia, which is also the world's fifth largest beer market.

Well-organized distribution channels have grown in recent years, especially in major urban centers, where some large-scale retail stores have recently emerged. Although such a situation greatly eases the task of bringing outside goods in to Russia, their location can oftentimes be sporadic. In some areas, much distribution takes place through informal channels like kiosks and open markets, making them extremely important for distributors.

St. Petersburg remains the main port of entry for a variety of consumer and industrial products for European Russia (Russia west of the Urals), while Vladivostok is the main port of entry for the Russian Far East. Generally, however, transportation infrastructure remains relatively underdeveloped, and most cargo moves by rail.

PRICING

Most Russian consumers are attracted to bargains and have relatively limited expendable incomes. However, many will pay for quality products, especially if they come from a well-known manufacturer. Low prices are therefore essential, since competitive prices are almost always offered by Russian and strong third-country competitors.

LEGAL REVIEW

JUDICIARY

Russia is a member of the International Center for the Settlement of Investment Disputes and accepts binding international arbitration. Foreign arbitration awards may be enforced in Russia, even if there is no reciprocal treaty between Russia and the country where the order was made. Russia is also a signatory to the 1958 New York Convention on the Recognition and Enforcement of Foreign Arbitral Awards.

However, despite recent improvements, Russia has a body of conflicting, overlapping and often rapidly changing laws, decrees and regulations, which result in a tendency towards unpredictability and confusion in doing business. Keeping up with legislative changes, presidential decrees and government resolutions is a challenging task. Uneven implementation of laws creates further complications; various officials, branches of government and jurisdictions interpret and apply regulations with little consistency, and the decisions of one may be overruled or contested by another.

Additionally, independent dispute resolution in Russia can be difficult to obtain since the judicial system is still developing. Meanwhile, court decisions are at times not executed. Therefore, many western attorneys refer their western clients who have investment or trade disputes in Russia to international arbitration in Stockholm or to courts abroad.

The Arbitration Court of the Russian Federation, which is part of the court system, is also available for arbitration purposes. As with international arbitral procedures, the weakness in the system is in Russian enforcement of decisions.

RIGHTS AND RESTRICTIONS FOR FOREIGN INVESTORS

Although federal law is uniform throughout Russia, it is often subject to local interpretation, a situation which those establishing a business should be aware of. New restrictions were recently approved in early 2007 limiting foreign access to more than 40 sectors of the national economy. These include military hardware, aviation and atomic energy, as well as foreign investments in oil and gas fields and mineral deposits that are deemed strategic. Several gold and copper fields will also be off limits to foreign investors. The regulations, which also clarify rules governing foreign investments in strategic Russian projects, have been part of a larger move by the Russian government to increase its role in key sectors of the economy.

The following basic laws and government resolutions regulate business registration in Russia: The 1999 Federal Law "On Foreign Investment in the Russian Federation", The 1999 Civil Code, the August 2001 Federal Law "On State Registration of Legal Entities" (entrepreneurs), Russian Government Resolution No. 319 "On Authorized Federal Entity of the Executive Power, Providing State Registration of Legal Entities" of May 2002, and a number of other legal acts. It is illegal to conduct a business without registration.

A bill "On Additional Measures to Attract Investments into Russian Automotive Industry Development" includes an exemption for foreign investors from customs duties on raw materials used for car assembly or production of spare parts. A land code allowing ownership by both local investors and foreigners of non-agricultural land was adopted in 2001, though some implementing regulations are still in development. The treatment of foreign investment in new privatizations is likely to remain inconsistent, while foreign investors participating in Russian privatization sales are often confined to limited positions.

The "Land Code" allows foreigners to buy non-agricultural land made available for private ownership and land not located near international borders, while under the "Agricultural Land Code," foreigners may lease agricultural land for 49 years.

INTELLECTUAL PROPERTY

Although Russia has made significant progress in improving the protection of Intellectual Property Rights (IPR), violations of IPR continue to be a problem. A report issued in January 2007 by such international corporate giants as General Electric, Vivendi Universal, EMI Group and Microsoft, accused Russia (along with China) of being the worst country worldwide for business piracy and counterfeiting "by a large margin." Lax government enforcement is cited as the primary cause of intellectual property theft.

Copyright piracy of films, videos, sound recordings, books and computer software can result in the loss of millions for investors, leading some film and music producers to sell DVDs and CVDs at lower prices in Russia to compete with local pirate products – a technique which has yet to show significant influence.

Many deficiencies remain in Russia's IPR regime, including a lack of explicit protection for test data for pharmaceutical products and agricultural chemicals and problems with law enforcement. Foreign firms need to take steps to protect their intellectual property, including registering their trademarks with the Russian Federal Service for Intellectual Property, Patents and Trademarks (Rospatent).

Despite the high rate of intellectual property theft, some efforts have been made by Russian authorities to deal with the matter. Russia has acceded to the Universal Copyright Convention, the Paris convention, the Berne convention, the Patent Cooperation Treaty, the Geneva Phonogram Convention, and the Madrid Agreement. The U.S.–Russia bilateral trade agreement mandates protection of the normal range of literary, scientific and artistic works through legislation and enforcement.

DUE DILIGENCE

Due diligence is extremely important for those wanting to establish a business in Russia, which can be a challenging market for foreign investors. The fact that the Russian economy is still in transition from a closed, socialist economy to a more open, market economy is also a major factor, since information about regulations, company ownership and credit worthiness is not always easy to find.

EXPROPRIATION

A 1991 investment code prohibits the nationalization of foreign investments except following legislative action and where deemed to be in the national interest. However, such nationalizations may be appealed to the courts of the Russian Federation.

Expropriation has been a problem at the sub-federal level, while local government interference or lack of enforcement of court rulings protecting investors has also been problematic.

STANDARDIZATION AND CERTIFICATION

The standards regime in Russia still lacks transparency despite significant improvements made in recent years, as Russia continues to rely on product testing for its product approval process. Plant auditing, quality systems, and post market vigilance remain underdeveloped. Restructuring of the former federal authority on standardization, Gosstandart, has also led to some uncertainty and confusion regarding standardization. The current authority for standardization, metrology and certification matters is the Federal Agency for Technical Regulations and Metrology under the jurisdiction of the Ministry of Industry and Energy.

As a result of such confusion, legal advice is extremely advisable for certification of products. The Department of Technical Regulations and

Metrology estimates that Russia must develop approximately 2,000 technical regulations by 2010. In recent years there has been a substantial movement toward the adoption of common international language on product standards and certification procedures for which some improvements have been made.

BUSINESS ETHICS

Corruption, crime, and sporadic business-related violence are not uncommon in Russia, especially in Moscow. Foreign investors considering establishing operations in the Russian market should take such issues into consideration. Since 2006, several high-profile businessmen and journalists have been killed in the country. Although much high-profile violence has occurred in the business world in Russia and has even become a norm in settling business disputes, it has yet to be directed at western executives specifically.

Corruption, however, is widespread, and western firms often encounter it. One view is that corruption stems from the belief by some Russian officials that foreigners will purchase Russian assets at below-market rates. This perception can at times impede bureaucratic approval for foreign investments. In addition, today's investors in Russia face the repercussions of the former Soviet system, whose thriving black-market permeated the economy at nearly every level and kept it afloat (Timofeyev, 1992). Russia ranks 126th on Transparency International's (TI's) 2005 Index (with a score of 2.4). Foreign firms have identified corruption as a pervasive problem, both in number of instances and in the size of bribes sought. Foreign entities should anticipate that since such a phenomenon is entrenched in Russian society, they should expect to be shaken down for protection money or solicited for bribes. This remains the case despite the fact that under the Russian Criminal Code (Articles 290 and 291), giving and receiving bribes is a criminal act carrying a prison sentence of up to 12 years. Russia has yet to criminalize the bribery of foreign officials however, thus there have been few high-profile, apolitical prosecutions that would send a clear deterrent message. Although President Putin has repeatedly stressed that enforcement of laws is a high priority of his administration, more transparent implementation of customs, taxation, licensing and other administrative regulations is necessary.

INVESTMENT OPPORTUNITIES

OIL AND GAS

Russia's oil and gas industry continues to prosper from growing production, sustained high oil prices and increasing exports. In the natural gas segment, local oil companies show increasing interest in becoming more involved in the market despite the position of Gazprom in the industry.

Oil and gas field machinery, oil recovery, exploration and field management services are expected to remain important exports to Russia, as well as services such as oil recovery, well optimization, horizontal drilling, hydrofracturing equipment and services, offshore development technologies and equipment, work-over, rehabilitation/reconditioning equipment/services as well as drilling and well tools and products, and idle well re-commissioning services.

Many Russian oil companies are increasing their capital expenditures on infrastructure and rehabilitation equipment and services, while foreign equipment, technological solutions and products for the industry are recognized for their excellent quality and after-sales service.

TELECOMMUNICATIONS

Driven by Russia's continuing strong economic performance, the Russian telecommunications market has continued to demonstrate strong growth, while the need to upgrade the generally inadequate telecommunications infrastructure throughout the country is also evident. Continued growth in the telecommunications services market will inevitably yield business opportunities for competitive foreign telecommunications equipment suppliers.

Revenue from cellular services represents the lion's share of the telecom services market. The number of cellular subscribers reached 120 million in 2005 and the penetration rate grew to 80 percent. Nearly 90 percent of the cellular communication market revenue belongs to three major national cellular operators: MobileTeleSystems (MTS), VympelCom and Megafon. Total revenue for fixed-line connection services reached $10.2 billion in 2005. The same year, the number of internet subscribers reached 18 million, while revenue for internet services increased to $1.5 billion.

Some of the best sales prospects for foreign investors is in digital switching equipment, high-speed, broadband internet access technologies, multi-service and multimedia solutions, including SDH, xDSL, ISDN, DWDM, BWA, and call center equipment. Companies entering the market should be prepared to compete with major foreign equipment manufacturers and deal with a complex regulatory environment.

The modernization of payphone systems in Russia is also considered an area with good promise, as payphone system modernization is a government level priority project.

COMPUTER HARDWARE AND SOFTWARE

Russia's computer market is driven mainly by new investments from the federal government into special economic zones and its new IT concepts. Most high-tech equipment is imported, while growth is expected to continue due to a favorable economic situation and high demand in the corporate and government sectors.

Many foreign firms are already operating in Russia, with products available either directly or through representatives or distributors. In 2005, the market for outsourcing software services was estimated at $1 billion. This market sector is maturing and new entrants will likely face serious competition from long-established companies. Government purchases, expansion of the IT market to Russia's regions and strong growth in mobile office sales were notable in the IT market in recent years.

Imports account for more than one-tenth of Russia's personal computer market, while peripherals, networking and larger system hardware are dominated by imports. Demand for legally imported operating systems, software application packages and enterprise management software is being driven by continuing growth in the number and purchasing power of small and medium-sized private enterprises.

Promising opportunities for sales of foreign manufactured hardware include data storage systems, networking equipment, PDAs and internet mobile technology.

AGRICULTURE

Russia is one of the fastest growing retail food sales markets in the world, with the potential to again double in size by 2008, just as it did since 2001. Retail sales of food and agricultural products have grown at an impressive rate reaching some $200 billion, of which approximately half are imported products. Simultaneously, retail outlets have begun to expand aggressively providing new potential markets for quality, imported goods and prospective venues for marketing programs. Moscow consumers continue to spend 70 percent of their incomes on consumer goods, which is the highest ratio in Europe (Interactive Research Group). The local food processing industry, as a result, has become one of the most dynamic sectors of the nation's economy, with an average increase of 15–20 percent annually, with processors willing to meet international quality standards and focus on quality ingredients.

With the participation of multinational retailers, quality now counts significantly in Russia's retail market. Demand has grown, therefore, for consumer ready products such as poultry, beef, pork, snacks, nuts, fresh and frozen fruits and vegetables, wine, beer, and seafood.

AGRICULTURAL MACHINERY

The Russian food and beverage market has experienced a boom in recent years due to an increase in consumer spending. As a result, agricultural spending has also increased, and is in need of significant modernization. It is estimated that the agricultural sector requires thousands of basic units, while some estimate that only around half of the needed machinery currently exists. In addition, it is estimated that approximately 80 percent of the current machinery requires upgrading, while the annual market demand for new agricultural machinery and equipment is approximately $3.5 billion. In the coming few years, Russian farmers are expected to need some 20,000 combines and 50,000 tractors annually.

Agromashholding and Rostselmash (Rostov-on-Don) manufacture approximately 90 percent (about 7,500 units) of all combines in Russia. In 2005, a number of Russian and German companies established joint ventures to assemble agricultural machinery in Russia such as Claas (Krasnodar), Kirovets-Landtechnik (St. Petersburg), and Eurotechnika (Samara). Recently several leading producers introduced new models of tractors and combines. Russian producers need to develop better quality agricultural equipment in order to compete with foreign suppliers. Furthermore, a supplier must be able to ensure reliable service and a supply of spare parts if used or refurbished equipment is to be bought.

As with many other sectors, however, there is a serious lack of financing for agricultural machinery purchases. Sellers who are able to provide financing, as well as a support system for purchases that go substantially beyond simple direct sales, or are willing to accept barter payments, have the greatest chance of securing deals in this sector.

In some cases though, financially healthy Russian companies are looking to expand to meet the growing demand for domestic food, creating opportunities for sales in areas such as grain processing equipment, fruit and vegetable processing equipment, dairy livestock breeding, swine and poultry production.

The Russian agricultural market is especially in need of items such as combines and other harvesting equipment, cultivators and other soil preparation equipment such as plows, harrows, cultivators, seeders, and fertilizer spreaders, and tractors.

CONSTRUCTION EQUIPMENT

The Russian Federal Government and regional governments invested $4.5 billion in important infrastructure and housing projects in 2005, while the nation's construction market has been growing at an average annual rate of approximately 10 percent over the past several years. Many private investors are actively increasing their operations in new housing and commercial real estate projects.

The average age of construction equipment is nearly 17 years old. Because local manufacturers have been unable to satisfy demand for new equipment for a number of reasons such as lack of modern technologies, insufficient investment in R&D and modernization, and poor management, the import market has grown more rapidly than the total market.

Price, reliability, availability of sales financing and after-sale service continue to be the main competitive factors limiting equipment exports to Russia. By offering state-of-the-art technology and products, and by employing reputable agents and/or distributors, foreign investors can ensure buyers for their products and services.

Equipment such as tower cranes, excavators, bulldozers, backhoe loaders, crushers and screens, concrete mixers and concrete pumps, asphalt pavers, spare parts and equipment leasing services for contractors are especially in need. Licensing and transferring modern technology to Russian equipment and component manufacturers also offer potential opportunities for investors.

MEDICAL EQUIPMENT

As a result of the expansion of Russia's health-care system, many opportunities have arisen with respect to the importation of medical equipment exports. There are nearly 10,000 hospitals in Russia, not including outpatient clinics and emergency treatment stations. There are also a significant number of health-care establishments which serve governmental entities such as the Ministry of Transportation, Ministry of Economic Development and Trade, and Ministry of Defense. A large portion of medical equipment and devices used in such clinics and hospitals is obsolete and needs replacement, and Russia relies exclusively on imports of such equipment.

Despite the great need for up-to-date equipment, financing remains insufficient to address the needs of the medical industry. However, in November 2005 President Putin announced health-care to be one of the four key national projects, along with education, housing and agriculture. One important promising development is the growth of health-care funding through massive federal investment and the development of health insurance systems. The Russian medical equipment and devices market has therefore shown substantial and steady growth over the past several years, with imports playing a significant role, accounting for some three-fourths of the total market. Russia is also dependent on a significant number of medical equipment industry sub-sectors, especially those requiring significant investments in R&D, innovative technologies, and automation.

Medical equipment which is in need in Russia includes: modern computerized diagnostic equipment, computer and X-Ray tomographs, angiography systems, resuscitation and functional diagnostic equipment, implants and prostheses, surgical and endoscopic equipment, headlights for surgeons, robotics clinical laboratory systems for express microanalysis, telemedicine complexes, hospital equipment and supplies, operational room equipment, artificial kidney complex components (oxigenerators and dialyzers), hospital beds, advanced home health-care equipment and supplies, and significant amounts of medical supplies and disposables, including polymeric packaging for IV solutions.

PHARMACEUTICALS

Over the past decade, the total volume of the market increased nearly ten-fold. Driven by rising incomes, consumer spending, increased efficiency in domestic distribution and increased government funding for drugs, annual growth in this sector is expected to continue to rise.

Russia has a growing pharmaceutical market with most major western drug manufacturers already represented in the country. The Russian pharmaceutical market is dominated by imported pharmaceuticals, which cover some 60 percent of the total volume.

The Russian pharmaceutical market presents good opportunities for foreign drug manufacturers, especially in the high-end quality product segment. Exports related to cardiovascular problems, cancer, asthma, neurological and hormonal problems, anti-AIDS drugs, insulin, antibiotics, analgesics, vitamins, vaccines, and psychotropic medicines are especially promising. Painkillers, antibiotics and vitamins remain top sellers in the Russian market, followed by medicines for heart and blood conditions, diabetes and liver problems.

AUTOMOBILES AND CAR PARTS

The Russian automotive market offers good opportunities for new car sales despite substantial import tariffs. By the end of 2006, the import market for new cars was expected to exceed 500,000 units. The market for car components and aftermarket replacement parts is likely to become stronger as car ownership steadily increases and customers demand higher performance from domestically produced cars. The Russian auto industry represents a major force in the domestic economy because of highly competitive pricing. There are several projects underway to assemble foreign cars in Russia. Ford's new plant began operation in 2002, with sales of Ford Focuses far exceeding demand. Recently, Renault began manufacturing a new low-cost Logan vehicle at a Moscow-based facility. Toyota also started construction of an assembly facility in St. Petersburg, which is projected to start manufacturing the Camry model in 2007.

However, the major obstacle to successful development of foreign assembly projects in Russia is the lack of local component suppliers. Engine and engine components, steering components, brake system components, powertrain components, seats, tires, interior components, and new car dealerships are in great need.

Good opportunities exist for foreign firms looking to establish local manufacturing facilities, form joint ventures with Russian firms, or supply components to foreign vehicle assembly projects in Russia. Another good prospect is to supply upgraded equipment and technology to Russian manufacturers. Opportunities also exist in the licensing and transferring of modern technology to Russian component manufacturers.

AIRCRAFT PARTS

Aircraft parts are increasingly in demand as Russian airlines continue to experience growth in passenger and cargo transportation. The Russian traffic market remains in certain sectors relatively immature, with strong potential for growth in both passenger and cargo sectors. Industry forecasts predict that in 2006–7 Russia's civil aviation market will experience an annual growth rate of 5.8 percent; currently, Russia's four major commercial airlines – Aeroflot, Sibir (S7), Pulkovo and UT Air – carry about 15 million passengers yearly. Russia's Ministry of Transport estimates that the Russian civil aviation sector demands from 2005 to 2010 will exceed 530 aircraft, including at least 180 new helicopters, 164 long-range aircraft and 146 regional aircraft.

Russia's aviation industry suffers from a lack of financing for aircraft construction and is in need of significant restructuring. For major Russian airlines, the necessity to update their fleet is beginning to outweigh the prohibitive nature of restrictive tariffs which have curbed such purchases thus far. The Russian government is considering lowering import tariffs on aircraft where there is no Russian equivalent. If import duties for aircraft are lowered, significant opportunities will arise for supply of aircraft, particularly used aircraft, spare parts, support and maintenance.

Russian government and industry representatives are looking for broader cooperation with foreign firms in order to revitalize their domestic industry and integrate it into the global aviation industry.

GENERAL INFORMATION

LANGUAGE

Many first-time visitors are surprised by how difficult it can be to find anyone who speaks English. Although many better-educated Russians in major cities speak English, knowing at least rudimentary Russian can be extremely helpful. One should hire a reputable interpreter for conducting important business negotiations.

LOCAL CUSTOMS

Oftentimes, Russian business people may come across as being cold or indifferent to their foreign counterparts. Despite such first impressions, the matter is one which is cultural and should not be something to be concerned about, but rather to get accustomed to. Russians, generally, are known for not smiling, though after becoming better acquainted they will tell you that they save their smiles for home.

Additionally, do not be off put by the fact that it may take days or weeks to receive responses to emails or telephone messages, resulting in extreme difficulty, at times, in scheduling meetings. A great deal of patience is many times required to confirm a date and time to meet after an initial agreement to set up an appointment. Hiring an interpreter is highly advised if one does not speak Russian. Most foreign businesspeople in Russia carry business cards in both Russian and English.

COMMUNICATION SERVICES

Russia has a relatively low level of internet penetration and awareness; approximately 15 percent of Russians use the internet on regular basis, 70 percent of whom use dial-up connection services. Wi-Fi is at the initial stages of its development in Russia, though is can be accessed at some 500 select locations, mainly in Moscow and St. Petersburg. Mobile services are provided in the GSM, CDMA-450, AMPS and DAMPS standards. GSM dominates the market.

RESIDENCY

Russian authorities require visas and residence permits for foreign investors. Work and residence permits must be renewed annually. At renewal times, such a process can be complicated as applicants may be required to reapply at a Russian embassy overseas. Travelers who arrive without an entry visa are subject to fines, delays, and/or deportation by route of entry at the traveler's expense. Visas, other than for transit purposes, are issued for those with a Russian sponsor, who is also responsible for applying for replacement, extension or changes to the visa. All foreigners must also have an exit visa to depart, which can either be issued along with an entry visa for short stays, or obtained by the sponsor after the traveler's arrival in the case of longer ones. Foreign citizens should carry their passport and visas with them at all times, as failure to present proper documentation can, at times, lead to fines or other steps.

TRANSPORTATION

Air travel in western Russia is generally on schedule though it can occasionally be erratic. In Russia's Far East, flights are less dependable, especially in the winter months. International Russian carriers such as Aeroflot and Transaero usually use western equipment. Most international flights enter Moscow through Sheremetyevo-2 and Domodedovo, two of the city's four major airports.

Train travel is highly recommended in Russia, and overnight rides from Moscow to St. Petersburg are generally reliable. One should be aware, however, of pickpockets. The metro in Moscow and St. Petersburg is efficient and inexpensive, though oftentimes crowded. Signs are in Russian only, so knowing the Cyrillic alphabet can be extremely helpful.

Short-term business travelers may wish to consider renting a car and driver for extensive excursions, or hire taxis through their hotels for shorter jaunts, though driving is less dependable due to Russia's weather conditions, poor road maintenance, and a culture of aggressive driving.

ACCOMMODATION

Although Moscow and St. Petersburg can offer world-class tourist facilities, other areas are often undeveloped, and one can find oneself regularly without water or electricity, a problem that can be especially troublesome in the minus-20 Farenheit weather in some areas. Other cities with western-style facilities are Novgorod, Nizhniy Novgorod, Nizhnevartovsk, Perm, Samara, Yekaterinburg, Perm, Sochi, Yuzhno Sakhalinsk and Vladivostok. Prices in such cities may be relatively high. In small cities, however, traditional Russian hotels offer modest accommodation at modest rates, though such rates may at times be raised for foreign guests. An increasing variety of relatively expensive restaurants are being established in large Russian cities, though the price of an average meal is generally quite high.

Russia is a predominately cash economy. It is illegal to pay for goods and services in foreign currency other than the ruble. Keep in mind that old, worn, or marked dollar bills may not be accepted at banks for exchange. Credit cards are accepted at very few stores, though they are now accepted at some modern businesses in Moscow and St. Petersburg, and at some hotels and restaurants in larger regional cities. Traveler checks are not widely accepted except in major cities.

SAFETY

Aside from minor theft, travel in Russia is fairly safe, except for Chechnya and the surrounding areas, where travel is not advised as it can be extremely dangerous. For those intending to make a trip to these regions, extreme caution must be used as some foreign visitors have been killed or kidnapped. Anyone traveling outside the main commercial centers is strongly urged to obtain up-to-date information about developments in the area they plan to visit.

HELPFUL RESOURCES – RUSSIA

GOVERNMENT AUTHORITIES

Ministry of Communications: http://english.minsvyaz.ru/enter.shtml
Ministry of Information Technologies and Communications:
    http://english.minsvyaz.ru/enter.shtml
Ministry of Industry and Energy: www.minprom.gov.ru
Ministry of Natural Resources: www.mnr.gov.ru
Ministry of Agriculture: www.mcx.ru
Ministry of Health and Social Development – Center for Sanitary and Epidemiological Norm-setting, Hygienic Certification and Expertise: www.crc.ru
Russian State Customs Committees: www.customs.ru or www.tks.ru
State Registration Chamber: www.palata.ru
Company Registration: www.mosnalog.ru
Russian Center for Tests and Certification: www.rostest.ru
Russian Standard: www.rosstandard.com

Federal Service for Control over Health-care and Social Development (Roszdravnadzor): www.roszdravnadzor.ru

Federal Construction and Housing Agency (Gosstroy): www.gosstroy.gov.ru

Federal Service for Control Over Health-care and Social Development: www.roszdravnadzor.ru

Federal Agency for Technical Regulations and Metrology: www.gost.ru

Federal State Enterprise Scientific Center for Testing Medical Products: www.regmed.ru

TRADE SHOWS

Svyaz Expocomm Moscow: http://www.ejkrause.com/events/3206.html

Golden Autumn, Agricultural Week Trade Show: www.apkvvc.ru/engaut.htm

Agroprodmash Trade Show: http://www-eng.expocentr.ru/expo

Construction and Material Handling Equipment Show: www.mst-expo.ru

Russian Road Equipment Show: www.doroga-expo.ru

Svyaz ExpoComm Trade Show: www.ejkrause.com

Cable & Satellite TV, Teleradiobroadcasting and Broadband Exhibition: www.cstb.ru/index_eng.php

AVIATION RELATED RESOURCES

Russian Aviation News & Information Server: www.avia.ru/english

International Aviation & Space Salon: www.airshow.ru/etable.htm

Rosaviaexpo: www.rosaviaexpo.ru

Sukhoi Civil Aviation: www.scac.ru

A Listing of Russian Airlines: www.polets.ru

MISCELLANEOUS

Black Sea Trade and Development Bank (BSTDB): www.bstdb.gr/bank.htm

European Bank for Reconstruction and Development: www.ebrd.org

The World Bank International Finance Corporation: www.infoexport.gc.ca/

Russian Franchise Association: www.rarf.ru/eng

International Finance Corporation: www.ifc.org

Kompaniya: http://ko.ru

BuyBrand: http://buybrand.ru/eng

Russian Institute for Comprehensive Information on Certification and Quality (VNIIKI): www.vniiki.ru

Research Institute for Certification (VNIIS): www.vniis.ru

Association of Oil and Gas Equipment producers: www.oil-gas.biz

Pharminform, specializing in assistance with registration and certification of medical equipment and pharmaceuticals: www.pharminform.ru

Chapter 2

Investing in Ukraine

❖   Marketing Strategies – 64
❖   Pricing – 65

LEGAL REVIEW – 65

❖   Judiciary – 65
❖   Rights and Restriction for Foreign Investors – 66
❖   Intellectual Property – 67
❖   Standardization and Certification – 68
❖   Business Ethics – 69

INVESTMENT OPPORTUNITIES – 69

❖   Construction and Regeneration – 69
❖   Pharmaceuticals and Medical Equipment – 70
❖   Agriculture and Agricultural Machinery – 70
❖   Pesticides – 71
❖   Food Processing and Packaging Equipment – 71
❖   Airport Equipment and Services – 72
❖   Security and Safety Equipment – 72
❖   Automotive Parts – 73
❖   Computer Software, Services and Accessories – 73
❖   IT and Telecommunications – 74
❖   Power Generation – 74
❖   Gas and Oil Field Machinery – 75
❖   Environmental Goods and Services – 75
❖   Leisure and Tourism – 76
❖   Retail – 76
❖   Public Procurement – 77

GENERAL INFORMATION – 77

❖   Language – 77
❖   Local Customs – 77
❖   Visas – 78
❖   Transportation – 78

LYING AT THE CROSSROADS OF RUSSIA, the Middle East and Eastern Europe, Ukraine is located at an important strategic location for investment in Eastern Europe. With quickly improving financial and political environments, Ukraine has made significant progress in recent years in developing its economy while opening its markets to foreign investment and exports. As a result, the Ukrainian economy is considered one of the most dynamic in Europe, having expanded at impressive rates in recent years. Ukraine boasts a skilled, educated and relatively cheap workforce, and an abundance of agricultural land and mineral reserves. In addition, Ukraine has a well-developed communications and transportation infrastructure, and nearly 48 million consumers. The Ukrainian economy is comprised of light and heavy industry, oil refining, oil and gas transit, coal and mineral extraction, chemicals, agriculture, and food processing to name a few. The list of potentially lucrative sectors for investment is long, while several potentially lucrative investment opportunities for foreign investors exists in energy efficiency, electrical power systems, oil & gas equipment, transportation infrastructure development, banking and commercial real estate. Additionally, the establishment of manufacturing sites serving customers of the European Union and Russia is also considered an important potential investment opportunity due to the country's strategic location.

Ukraine enjoys most favored nation status with the EU, and is a party to the 1995 CIS free trade agreement, making it an attractive destination for many investors. Ukraine also has a Partnership and Co-operation Agreement (PCA) with the European Union. Additionally, free trade agreements have been signed with the entire former Soviet republics except Tajikistan, and it participates in the Black Sea Cooperation Council. It has also concluded trade agreements granting most favored nation status to export – import operations with Austria, Argentina, Armenia, Bulgaria, Canada, Estonia, Finland, Krygzstan, Latvia, Moldova, Russia and Switzerland. Ukraine intends to become a full member of the Central European Free Trade Agreement (CEFTA) after ascension to the World Trade Organization. Membership to the WTO has been a longtime goal of Ukraine, and in 1993 it presented its application for membership to the organization. Ukraine is currently in the process of negotiation for ascension.

In an effort to strengthen Ukraine's economy and improve the nation's investment climate, a series of steps has been undertaken in recent years, including deregulation, activation of a free stock market, clarification of the National Bank's decision on regulating foreign investment, establishing clear rules regarding capitalization, reinforcing the independence of courts, and reviving free economic zones, technology parks and priority development areas. The results of such steps have so far proven positive for Ukraine, with high growth of key banking indices already drawing the attention of foreign investors. Indeed, the number of joint ventures with foreign entities in Ukraine is growing, with international names such as Tambrand, Pratt & Whitney, Proctor & Gamble, and others included in the list of success stories. In most cases Ukrainian partners provided manufacturing space, labor, energy and expertise in the complexities of dealing with local bureaucracy. Foreign firms contributed technology, equipment and product know-how. In addition, the consumer sector, trade, real estate and non-banking financial institutions are also expected to maintain their current growth levels and attract a growing number of investors.

POLITICAL BACKGROUND

POLITICAL STRUCTURE

Ukraine has a presidential, parliamentary, multi-party government with separate executive, judicial, and legislative branches. The prime minister is nominated by the president, and must be confirmed by the parliament. The president is elected by popular vote for a five-year term, and is responsible for choosing a foreign and defense minister; the prime minister elects the Cabinet of Ministers selected.

The "Supreme Rada" is the nation's unicameral parliament body, which has 450 members and initiates legislation, ratifies international agreements, and approves the budget. Up until 2006, half of the parliament was chosen by proportional vote from party lists and half from individual constituencies. Today, all seats are chosen from party lists. Ukrainian political blocs represent a wide range of ideologies from ultra-nationalist conservative to leftist and include former communists, socialists, agrarians, liberals, nationalists, as well as centrists groups.

KEY FIGURES

Ukraine's president and chief of state is elected by popular vote for a five-year term. As of January 2005, Viktor A. Yushchenko has served as the nation's president after being supported by the Ukrainian public in a series of peaceful protests termed the "Orange Revolution," which resulted in the reversal of a fraudulent presidential election in 2004–5. The Cabinet of Ministers, which exercises executive power, is headed by the Prime Minister Viktor Yanukovich. Borys I. Tarasyuk serves as the country's foreign minister, Vladimir Stelmakh is the Governor of the Central Bank, and Stanislav Stashevskyy is the first Deputy Prime Minister.

POLITICAL DEVELOPMENTS AND FOREIGN RELATIONS

Following the dissolution of the USSR and a referendum on independence which was approved by 90 percent of the popular vote, Ukraine became independent in 1991. Ukraine later helped co-found the Commonwealth of Independent States (CIS) and Ukraine became the first nation to adopt a post-Soviet constitution at the time. Democracy, economic reform and privatization, however, remained challenging principles to implement in the new independent country. Additionally, in 1992 ethnic tensions in Crimea prompted a number of pro-Russian organizations to advocate the annexation of Crimea to Russia. Ultimately, though, the region remained under Ukrainian control.

At the end of 2004, the mass public protests of tens of thousands of Ukrainians during the Orange Revolution forced the authorities to overturn a fraudulent presidential election which included government intimidation and expulsion of the opposition and of independent media, multiple voting by busloads of voters, abuse of state administrative resources, skewed media coverage and other provocations. The demonstrations culminated in the rise to power of reformist Viktor Yushchenko, who was inaugurated on January 23, 2005. The new Yushchenko government has sought to maintain good relations with Russia while declaring Euro-Atlantic integration to be a top priority.

Despite the fact that in December 1991 Ukraine co-founded the Commonwealth of Independent States (CIS), in January 1993 it refused to endorse a draft charter among CIS member states strengthening political, economic, and defense ties between them. Ukraine is also a founding member of the Georgia–Ukraine–Uzbekistan–Azerbaijan–Moldova alliance, GUUAM. In 1945 Soviet Ukraine joined the United Nations as one of its original members following a western compromise with the Soviet Union, which asked for seats for all of its 15 union republics. From 1999 to 2001 Ukraine served as a non-permanent member of the UN Security Council, and has made significant contributions to UN peacekeeping operations since 1992. In January 1992 Ukraine joined the then-Conference on Security and Cooperation in Europe, later to become the Organization for Security and Cooperation in Europe (OSCE), and then joined the North Atlantic Cooperation Council later that year. In 1997 the country signed a Charter Agreement with NATO and expressed interest in membership. It later sent troops to Kosovo in cooperation with NATO countries and signed an agreement for NATO use of Ukrainian strategic airlift assets; it is the most active member of the Partnership for Peace (PfP). The European Union's Partnership and Cooperation Agreement (PCA) with Ukraine went into effect in 1998. However, after the 2004 round of EU expansion, Ukraine was not chosen for an association agreement, to its disappointment. Instead, it was included in a "neighbor" policy. NATO offered Ukraine an "Intensified Dialogue on Membership Issues" in 2005.

In terms of current foreign relations, Ukraine maintains peaceful relations with all its neighbors, especially Poland and Russia, though energy relations and boundaries in the Sea of Azov and the Kerch Strait have at times complicated relations with the latter. Some unresolved maritime issues remain along the Danube and in the Black Sea with Romania, while the 1997 boundary treaty with Belarus remains unratified due to unresolved financial claims. However, there are no armed conflicts in the country and nearly no security risks. Moldova and Ukraine have established joint customs posts to monitor transit through Moldova's Transnistria Region, which remains under OSCE supervision. Ukraine participated in the five-sided talks on the conflict in Moldova and supported a non-military resolution to conflict in post-Soviet Georgia.

High political uncertainty came with the nation's parliamentary elections in March 2006, which ultimately led to the formation of a majority coalition and a new government. The leading party in the race was the Party of Regions (Partiya Rehioniv), followed by the Yuliya Tymoshenko Bloc (Blok Yuliy Tymoshenko). A portion of power formerly reserved for the president was also transferred in 2006 to the parliament, making Ukraine a parliamentary – presidential democracy but also adding to the risk of inter-institutional struggle and occasional political paralysis. Despite the upheaval, prospects remained good for the country and its economy.

ECONOMIC REVIEW

BACKGROUND, FORECASTS AND RISKS

Ukraine has a well-developed industrial and scientific base. It has managed and maintained powerful heavy industry and mechanical engineering sectors despite the fact that upon declaring independence, more than 80 percent of its industrial enterprises required radical reconstruction and overhaul. The government's decision to implement a much more open fiscal approach to the nation's economy seems to be paying off. Rapid growth in industry, especially

Table 2.1   State Budget, 2006 (UAH bn)

Expenditure	137.1
Revenue	124.9
Balance	12.2
As percent of GDP	2.5

Source: Press reports, Economic Intelligence Unit Country Report January 2006, <www.eiu.com>.

Table 2.2   Basic Indicators of Social and Economic Development in
             Ukraine

	2006	Nov./06–Dec./06	Dec./05–Dec./06	2005–2006	2004–2005
GDP mln. UAH	–	–	–	107.0	102.7
Industrial output sold (work, services) mln. UAH	413,082.9	–	–		
Industrial production index		102.2	112.0	106.2	103.1
Agricultural output, mln. UAH	94,300	–	–	100.4	99.9
Exports of goods, mln. USD	34,676.7	–	–	111.4	105.6
Imports of goods, mln. USD	39,899.6	–	–	122.4	125.1
Balance, mln. USD	–5,222.9	–	–		
Retail trade turnover, mln. UAH	226,918.4	–	–	124.8	122.4
Household expenditures, mln. UAH	378,423	100.1	126.4	132.4	132.2
Arrears in wages and salaries, mln. UAH	806.4	81.0	84.0	–	86.4
Of which from budget funds	0.5	1.4	157.3	–	17.7
Industrial producer price index	–	100.5	114.1	114.1	109.5
Consumer price index	–	100.9	111.6	111.6	110.3

Source: State Statistics Committee of Ukraine, <http://www.ukrstat.gov.ua>.

in export-related metallurgy and chemicals, helped maintain impressive economic performance. Ukraine's economy in 2006 expanded 7 percent on the year, faster than the government had anticipated, with healthy exports of steel, its major export commodity, contributing significantly to the impressive expansion. Previously, in 2005, Ukraine's economy expanded 2.7 percent on the year as world steel prices dropped, thus reducing demand for Ukrainian steel exports. Ukraine's 2006 GDP amounted to $95.1 billion, while its per capita GDP reached $2,041. Its real GDP growth in 2007, according to government authorities, is expected to accelerate to at least 5 percent, with year-end inflation at the end of 2007 expected to slow to 8 percent. The

Table 2.3   Forecast Summary, 2007 (percentage)

Real GDP growth	5.0
Industrial production growth	6.0
Gross fixed investment growth	9.0
Average unemployment rate	4.2
Average consumer price inflation	9.0
Commercial bank lending rate	14.0
Consolidated government balance (percent of GDP)	2.0
Exports of goods fob (US$ bn)	41.9
Imports of goods fob (US$ bn)	41.9
Current-account balance (US$ bn)	0.5
Current-account balance (percent of GDP)	0.5
External debt (year-end; US$ bn)	29.2

Source: Economic Intelligence Unit Country Report January 2006 – Ukraine, <www.eiu.com>.

national currency, the Ukrainian hryvnia (UAH) is expected to remain broadly stable in nominal terms against the US dollar in 2006–7, with only a slight appreciation. The current-account surplus is expected to diminish considerably as well in 2006–7. However, the International Monetary Fund forecasts that Ukraine's GDP will grow 4–4.5 percent in 2007 and that inflation will exceed 10 percent. Recent data published by the Ukrainian Finance Ministry revealed that borrowing volume to the state budget in 2006 reached UAH 11.2. billion, while the extreme volume of public foreign debt of Ukraine is expected to reach $9.890 billion by the end of 2007.

Despite disappointments at the slow pace of reform, analysts maintain that privatization sales are likely to become more transparent in the country and fiscal policy will be rationalized. In addition, energy sector reform is expected to advance and corporate governance to improve. In general, it is expected that authorities will make a concerted effort to bring businesses out of the shadow economy. Higher investment-related spending is also anticipated. However, growth in social commitments in 2007 is expected to slow considerably in the absence of electoral considerations. Analysts expect the budget deficit to remain at around 2 percent of the GDP. Adequate financing is anticipated as a result of privatization earnings along with foreign and domestic borrowing.

The National Bank of Ukraine (NBU) places great emphasis on the need for price stability and is expected to keep the hyvnya stable despite the fact that the possibility of some currency weakening exists due to the growing trade deficit and the sharp increase in the price paid for Russian gas imports. The

NBU is expected to periodically tighten some aspects of its monetary policy as a result, such as the reserve requirements of commercial banks. Investment will likely be encouraged in 2007, while, despite slow income growth, household consumption is expected to remain strong, standing at around 8.9 percent year-on-year in real terms.

Ukraine is expected to benefit from an anticipated drop in the cost of oil imports in 2007, though investment will be dampened by several factors including the hike in the gas price by Russia. Steel prices are set to fall further. Another major development to affect the Ukrainian economy came three days after the Russian gas monopoly, Gazprom, reduced supplies of gas to Ukraine and western Europe on January 4, 2007. It was then that the Russian and Ukrainian sides reached a five-year agreement on new terms for their gas trade, both on the sale of gas to Ukraine and the transit of Russian gas via Ukraine to EU states. After a somewhat lengthy battle over the guidelines of the two countries' interests, Ukraine ultimately moved towards market prices for gas, a painful yet positive step for the country. Doing so will reduce the distortions in Ukraine's economy and lead to sharply lower gas consumption in addition to reducing the scope for corruption and the leverage that Russia has over Ukraine. Recent data released by Ukrainian authorities predicts that the investment capacity of the energy sector of Ukraine will reach some $200 billion through 2030 with annual capital investments to energy-saving programs stepped up several times until then. In the meantime, the country's priority remains securing the parallel works of the Ukrainian and European energy systems. By the end of the decade, Ukraine is expected to implement 22 investment projects in the power industry with at least $1.4 billion. In addition, the World Bank's 2004–7 Country Assistance Strategy (CAS) is attempting to support the country's aspirations to join the EU.

BUSINESS ENVIRONMENT

OVERVIEW

Ukraine is the second largest country in Europe with a population of approximately 48 million people. Following independence in 1991 and subsequent economic decline, Ukraine's economy began growing at the end of 1999 and has been expanding since. Significant liberalization steps have been taken by Ukrainian authorities over the past few years, including reduced regulation, elimination of most licensing requirements as well as most restrictions on foreign exchange. Ukraine's economic performance has been strong and poverty has declined dramatically since 2000. Its GDP grew by more than 50 percent from 1999 to 2004, which, along with significant improvement in the country's fiscal position, led to an impressive drop in Ukraine's debt-to-GDP ratio. Ukraine's export-driven economy has grown at impressive rates in recent years; in January – October 2004, exports totaled $26.5 billion, reflecting a 43.3 percent growth rate. Imports also grew during the same period by some 28 percent, reaching $23.3 billion. However, since its economy depends so heavily on exports, the Ukrainian regulatory system is structured to promote export while protecting Ukraine's local market from competitors wishing to import products into the country. As a result, importers oftentimes face frustrating customs, certification and licensing procedures when trying to import goods into Ukraine.

Local companies, meanwhile, face high taxation rates and at times iniquitous collection of taxes. Such circumstances can make investment difficult and have resulted in gaps between the economic progress of Ukraine and some of its neighbors in the Eastern European region. Unfair competitive practices have also been a major impediment to doing business in Ukraine. Competitors in the shadow economy who do not pay taxes fully along with businesses favored by local authorities hinder healthy competition. Despite Ukraine's anti-monopoly policy and consumer protection legislation, around 3,000 violations of the anti-monopoly legislation were recorded in 2004. The Ukrainian market has been flooded with products of poor quality and often mislabeled under well-known western brand-names; however, Ukrainian food and alcohol products are generally of excellent quality. Therefore, contradictory attitudes regarding foreign products in Ukraine should be taken into account when beginning a business venture.

Major superstores recently established in Ukraine have already begun shifting the business landscape of the country; these stores, present in major cities, either specialize in consumer electronics or food products, while other goods are sold in specialized retail outlets or open markets. Such a situation

Table 2.4   Risk Ratings, 2006

Category	Current Score*	Previous Score
Security risk	46	46
Political stability risk	55	75
Legal and regulatory risk	73	73
Tax policy risk	50	50
Labor market risk	54	54
Infrastructure risk	75	78
Overall risk assessment	59	62

Source: Economist Intelligence Unit, Ukraine Risk Briefing 2006.
*(100=highest risk)

Table 2.5   Joint Venture Case Study

Company: Isuzu Automotive Company, Ukraine
Shareholders: Isuzu 30 percent, Bogdan 50 percent, Sojitz 20 percent
Date of establishment: April 2006
Capital stock: 25 million hryvnia ($4.95 million)
Main business: Sales of Isuzu trucks, Bogdan buses

Company developments:
Since 1999, Bogdan has produced or sold light-duty buses using the platform of the Isuzu ELF light-duty truck. Sales in the market of buses manufactured by Bogdan have rapidly expanded since then, mainly due to the high quality of the product.

Shipments of Isuzu ELF increased from 9 units in 1999 to 1,610 units in 2003, to 3,123 units in 2005.

Isuzu aims to supply Bogdan with 20,000 units yearly in the future, including exports to Ukraine's neighboring countries.

Source: Isuzu Motors Ltd., www.isuzu.co, local press reports.

creates an environment in which retailers either target rich or poor customers, while an expanding middle class must choose between pricey boutiques or open markets. Meanwhile, a growing number of Ukrainians with rising income levels can opt for high-quality, name-brand goods. Additionally, as a result of having experienced significant financial crises combined with limited opportunities for long-term savings or investments, many Ukrainians spend their relatively meager earnings on high-cost goods including jewelry, furniture, clothing and household appliances whenever they can, since alternative investment options continue to be extremely limited.

PRIVATIZATION

In 1999, mass privatization of small and medium-scale enterprises was completed, leaving most of these businesses in private hands. The result has been significant economic growth, for in 2004 privatization receipts reached $1.7 billion, higher than in any previous year. Shares of thousands of privatized enterprises served as the basis for the establishment of stock exchanges and an over-the-counter trading system. However, lack of clear regulatory control has impeded the government's ability to privatize enterprises in several key sectors.

The cash sale of majority shareholdings in several strategic enterprises, open bidding procedures, and the use of financial advisers to assist Ukraine's State Property Fund (SPF), are provided by a somewhat transparent privatization law. However, much remains to be desired in terms of privatization transparency. Despite the fact that in theory equal treatment is provided both foreign and domestic investors under privatization rules, foreign participation is limited for certain strategic enterprises such as radio, television, energy and insurance. Additionally, weak regulations have allowed Ukrainian and sometimes Russian business interests to circumvent privatization rules. Private enterprises in Ukraine also face significant regulatory burdens from the Ukrainian government despite deregulation steps taken. Numerous required certificates and inspection regimes continue to exist, while the State Committee for Regulatory Policy and Entrepreneurial Activity (SCRPEA) is required to asses the possible impact on entrepreneurial activity of all proposed new laws, ministerial decrees and regulations before they are adopted.

In addition, some owners of privatized Ukrainian companies have expressed fear of possible re-privatization in the future. The government, however, has responded to such claims by saying that there are no grounds for mass nationalization or re-privatization, except when companies are privatized in violation of law, a move that can be made only through the court.

MAJOR TRADE PARTNERS, PRODUCTS AND TRENDS

Ukraine's exports constitute approximately 60 percent of the nation's GNP, twice the average of most national economies and more than its neighbors in the EU, including Poland. In recent years, metal, and especially steel, has contributed to more than half of Ukraine's exports. With steel exports reaching all-time highs and global steel prices rising, such exports have significantly aided the country's economic growth and export boom in 2004. Additionally, 39 percent of exports consist of non-precious metals and related products, while minerals, chemicals, food, crops, textiles, machinery, transport equipment and vehicles account for 49 percent. More than 36 percent of imports consist of oil and gas.

The country's abundant uranium-ore deposits represent an important draw for foreign investors, especially as world prices continue to rise and shortages are foreseen in the future. Recent reports claim that Ukraine has enough uranium reserves to substantially reduce Russian imports and fill domestic demand for up to a millennium. Dozens of foreign firms have therefore sought entry into the market to gain control over uranium mining, as well as the process to convert it into nuclear fuel. Ukrainian authorities, however, have chosen to yield monopoly control over the precious ore, keeping foreign investors at a distance in the meantime. The state-owned VostGOK currently controls the Ukrainian uranium extraction industry, extracting some 800 tons annually, though according to the nation's Energy Minister Yuriy Boyko it hopes to nearly double domestic uranium production by 2009. At present, most of Ukraine's domestically mined uranium is exported to Germany. In the meantime, many companies continue to vie for whatever portion of the sector they can control, including France's Areva NP and Australia's Uran Limited.

Roughly one-third of Ukraine's exports go to Europe, one-third to the CIS, and one-third to other countries. Russia accounts for 18 percent of Ukrainian exports of some $5 billion and 41.2 percent of Ukrainian imports making it Ukraine's largest trading partner. The Netherlands has also proven to be a major investor in the Ukrainian economy, taking the third position amongst investors in the country in 2006. There are 306 Ukrainian – Dutch joint ventures in Ukraine.

Destinations for Ukrainian exports include Germany (the largest destination in Europe), Poland, Hungary, the US, China and Turkey, with which Ukraine has the largest trade surplus, followed by Italy and Romania. Imports to Ukraine come from Germany, Poland, Turkmenistan, Italy, the US, China, and the UK

BANKING

At the head of Ukraine's banking system is the National Bank of Ukraine (NBU), the nation's central bank responsible for registration of commercial banks and oversight of their activities and monetary circulation. The NBU also moderates changes in the exchange rate. Nearly 200 other commercial banks also operate in Ukraine, several of which have 100 percent foreign capital. From 2005 to 2006, the share of foreign capital in the statutory capital of Ukrainian banks grew from 19.5 percent to 27.6 percent. This figure is expected to continue to grow in coming years.

During the first three months of 2007, several other foreign banks expressed keen interest in the Ukrainian market. During the same period Austria's Volksbanken-AG (ÖVAG) extended its network to Ukraine; a confidentiality agreement was signed with the National Bank of Greece, which expressed a non-binding interest and is exploring the potential for investing in two banks in Ukraine; and the Swedbank banking group of Sweden signed an agreement to buy TAS-Kommerzbank in Ukraine for $753 million.

The top ten banks in the county control more half of all outstanding loans and own nearly 40 percent of all capital in the system. The banking sector plays a small role in Ukraine's economy as total bank assets remain relatively small, with the country remaining in the "poor" category in the standard rankings of deposits. Most banks have a high cost structure combined with low operating profits. Foreign licensed banks may carry out the same activities as domestic banks, and can operate via subsidiaries in Ukraine. Companies with no representation in Ukraine may not open deposit accounts with Ukrainian banks. However, a bank account may be opened to conduct settlements if necessary. In general, Ukraine remains a cash economy, but this trend is slowly changing.

CURRENCY

Ukraine's currency, the hryvnia (UAH), was introduced in 1996, has floated freely since 2000 and has been fairly stable. Strong currency policy and successful management of the external debt-service obligations have enabled such stability, especially as the currency switched to an openly floating exchange rate. In general, the hryvnia has been stable against the dollar in recent years but has declined against the Euro.

Unhindered transfer of profits and revenues in foreign currency is guaranteed by Ukraine's "Foreign Investment Law" of 1996. However, foreign investments can only be conducted in hryvnia since such investment funds can only be brought into Ukraine via special commercial bank accounts which must convert hard currency into hryvnia. Additionally, all payments to foreign investors must be made in hryvnia to bank accounts in Ukraine. Foreign currency loans may be received by resident legal entities and entrepreneurs and foreign banks. Hard currency received by a purely Ukrainian company is subject to a 50 percent conversion requirement, while a license must be obtained by the NBU for some operations. Foreign investors, meanwhile, may repatriate earnings. However, a fee is required for transactions of over $50,000 in hard currency being sent out of Ukraine, which must be initially approved by the NBU. Ukraine residents, on the other hand, may only transfer up to $300 abroad without opening a bank account. If a company wishes to make a transaction greater than $10,000, permission must be acquired from the State Tax Administration; if it wishes to purchase hard currency, a copy of the foreign trade contract must be presented to banks.

TAXATION AND CUSTOMS DUTIES

General lack of predictability and transparency prevails, with the most common complaints from businesses in Ukraine involving tax administration. One key issue is the administration of refunds to exporters for VAT that has been collected; there is a large backlog of refunds that must be repaid, a topic which is being discussed with Ukrainian authorities and the IMF. There has also been discrimination against foreign companies in the use of promissory notes to cover VAT for temporary imports. In addition to confusing regulations and a heavy tax burden, investors complain of harassment by tax officials, discriminatory applications, and disproportionate penalties. Imports from western countries, however, are usually given preferential tariff rates, depending on the type of products imported. Generally, if a product similar to that being imported is also produced in the local market, the rate of taxation will be higher. Under the guidelines of Ukraine's international agreements on prevention of double taxation, Ukrainian authorities approved a tax exemption on profits of non-Ukrainians whose home nations have signed bilateral agreements with Ukraine against double taxation and who pay taxes on repatriated profits.

In all, there are 22 types of national taxes under Ukraine's tax system. Of these, principal taxes and compulsory payments are required of the following: corporate profits tax, value added tax (VAT), personal income tax, pension charge, excise tax, land tax, tax on owners of motor vehicles, stamp duty, charge on environmental pollution, royalties for extraction of oil, natural gas and gas condensate, charge for the use of radio frequency and a charge for guaranteeing bank deposits of individuals. Parliament has tried on several occasions to reduce the VAT rate from 20 percent to 17 percent, though the move has always been blocked. Currently, goods exempt from VAT include raw materials, component parts, equipment, machinery, and energy for production purposes and the enterprise's own needs. Additionally, import of materials and equipment and exports of domestically produced spacecraft and equipment are also exempt until 2009, while goods used for the development of the domestic car construction industry and exports of domestically produced or assembled cars and components are also exempt from VAT until 2008. Materials and equipment used for the development of certain chemicals and for the ammunition production industry are exempt until 2010.

All imports into Ukraine are subject to customs duty, which range from 2 percent to 50 percent. This rule does not apply to foreign investors who contribute foreign investment to a Ukrainian resident company's in return for ownership rights in the firm. Excise taxes can range from 5 percent to 300 percent, depending on whether or not the taxed item is a product of Ukraine. Imports of a number of foreign agricultural products are banned by Ukraine, which cites reasons of food safety. Dried-egg products, for instance, are prohibited due to fears of salmonella. Other products are generally not restricted, while Ukrainian importers often find ways to circumvent existing import restrictions, especially through Special Economic Zones. The following documents are necessary for importation: the signed contract; certificate of origin of goods; cargo customs declaration with the description and value of goods, term of payment and terms of shipment as well as import licenses on certain goods on cosmetics and hygiene products, agricultural chemicals, pharmaceutical products and veterinary medicines, ozone-depleting substances, and industrial-grade polycarbonate. Most import licenses are granted through the Ministry of Economy. The State Customs Service of Ukraine (SCS) has free access to companies' premises where commodities subject to customs clearing are stored. In addition, the SCS can check the financial and economic performance of such companies.

In compliance with Ukraine's international agreements on prevention of double taxation, authorities approved a tax exemption on profits of non-Ukrainians who pay taxes on repatriated profits and whose home nations have signed bilateral agreements with Ukraine against double taxation. However, there remains a risk that taxes will be enforced in a manner that favors local firms despite the fact that the laws, in theory, are non-discriminatory. Risk to foreign investors also comes from sudden changes in the tax environment that leave businesses little time to adjust.

Several years ago, special incentives granted to foreign investors were abolished. Most recently, the Budget Law of 2005 and Other Laws No. 2505 did away with certain favorable tax and customs stipulations. Meanwhile, the country has also entered into investment protection treaties with a large number of countries in order to protect foreign investors against certain restrictions and for the protection of losses resulting from expropriation. On December 24, 2002 the Parliament voted to reform the "Enterprise Profits Tax," cutting the corporate tax rate from 30 percent to 25 percent and liberalizing provisions for loss carryovers. A flat rate of 13 percent on personal income was introduced in 2004.

FREE/SPECIAL ECONOMIC ZONES

As of December 2004, there were 11 Special Economic Zones (SEZs) and 11 priority development Areas (PDA), offering tax and import duty exemptions and other benefits to encourage investment and production of goods for export. Such areas differ by tax concessions granted. Free Economic Zones (FEZs) mandate privileges for 10 to 30 years (depending on the investment). Priority Development Territories (PDT) do not have independent customs borders. There is a moratorium on creation of new SEZs, which was again violated by the creation of new zones, two of which were created in November 2003. The IMF and World Bank suggested that the zones be eliminated and advised the government to focus instead on improving the overall investment climate in the country. The Ukrainian government did cancel some previously granted privileges, but formidable regional political interests are likely to prevent closure of the FEZs.

Ukraine has 20 seaports and 10 river ports. All river ports are open or closed joint stock companies, are under the authority of the Ministry of Transportation's Department of Sea and River Transport, and are state-run. Porto-Franco in Odessa has the status of a free port.

LABOR AND WAGES

Ukraine has a well-educated and skilled labor force with nearly a 100 percent literacy rate. However, there remains a shortage of managers and employees with exposure to doing business in a market economy. As of 2005, unemployment stood at around 7.6 percent, alongside considerable underemployment. Previous government demands to maintain employment levels are decreasing, though foreign investors may face government resistance to trimming the workforce to an efficient level. Labor market risk is low, with strikes common only in the state sector and rarely affecting foreign firms. Labor laws in Ukraine are generally tilted in favor of employees and against the employer. Despite their training, Ukrainian workers generally fail to demonstrate significant initiative as they are accustomed to "top-down" management practices. More independent-minded youth are entering the workforce, however, thus making it easier to find workers who function independently. Professional personnel can be accessed through several local and international recruitment agencies working in Ukraine.

Wages in Ukraine are very low by western standards. Wage compensation is slowly moving away from a system that compensates on the basis of age to one in which productivity is paramount. Freedom of association in Ukraine is respected. Financial and credit sectors offer the highest wages while agricultural workers receive the lowest wages. According to Ukrainian legislation, the minimum wage is adjusted whenever consumer price increases reach 5 percent. The government announced that by 2007 the minimum wage in the country would reach the subsistence level, which was increased to UAH 423 per month in January 2005. Payroll taxes (both employee-paid and employer-paid) total over 40 percent of wages.

Working time is limited to 40 hours a week, and though an employer may introduce a six-day working week, the maximum hours per day may not exceed seven hours. The minimum annual holiday entitlement is 24 calendar days, though a holiday may be longer depending on the number of years worked, working conditions and the employee's position. Retirement age is 55 years for women and 60 years for men.

FOREIGN DIRECT INVESTMENT

Despite macroeconomic successes and economic reforms in Ukraine which have improved the investment climate considerably, levels of foreign direct investment (FDI) to Ukraine do not match those enjoyed by neighboring Central European countries. Issues of corruption, transparency, and rule of law continue to impede full foreign investment potential for the country.

According to the Statistics Committee of Ukraine, total FDI into the country in 2005 was more than $9 billion, a relatively low level in the CIS. Annual FDI in Ukraine's neighbor, Poland, for example, is around 10 times that of Ukraine. The number of FDI projects, however, continues to grow in number.

MARKETING GOODS AND SERVICES

ESTABLISHING A BUSINESS

Keeping in mind that banks and insurance companies are heavily regulated and therefore must be established in compliance with specific requirements, four main options exist for establishing a business in Ukraine: a joint stock

Table 2.6   Foreign Direct Investments in Ukraine

Year	Number of FDI Projects	Capital Investments
2006	123	$1.91 billion
2005	124	$4.07 billion
2004	84	$1.2 billion
2003	71	$2.11 billion

Source: Loco Monitors, <www.locomonitor.com>.

Table 2.7   Country Sources of Ukraine Investment since 2002

Country Source	Number of Projects	Portion of Overall Investment
Russia	71	20 %
Germany	35	10 %
United States	35	10 %
Poland	30	9 %
Austria	22	6 %
Other	157	45 %

Source: Loco Monitors, <www.locomonitor.com>.

Table 2.8   FDI Projects in Ukraine by Category

Industry Category	Number of Projects	Portion of Overall Investment
Business & Financial Services	80	19 %
Light Industry	56	13 %
Food/Beverages/Tobacco	54	13 %
Heavy Industry	54	13 %
Infrastructure	48	11 %
Property, Tourism & Leisure	38	9 %
Transport Equipment	32	7 %
Consumer Products	19	4 %
Logistics & Distribution	17	4 %
Electronics	16	4 %
Other	16	4 %

Source: Loco Monitors, <www.locomonitor.com>.

Table 2.9   Business Function of Major FDI Projects in Ukraine

Business Function	Number of Projects	Portion of Overall Investment
Manufacturing	129	30 %
Retail	80	19 %
Business Services	76	18 %
Sales, Marketing	65	15 %
Construction	21	5 %
Logistics & Distribution	21	5 %
Internet or ICT Infrastructure	18	4 %
Research & Development	9	2 %
Extraction	8	2 %
Maintenance	2	0 %
Other	1	0 %

Source: Loco Monitors, <www.locomonitor.com>.

company, a limited liability company, a wholly-owned subsidiary, and a representative office. If a company plans to carry out manufacturing or other significant local commercial activities, a wholly owned company is recommended. A representative office, on the other hand, can carry out marketing, promotional, and other preparatory and supportive functions on behalf of the company. Such an establishment will generally be treated as an independent legal entity for regulatory and taxation purposes. No prohibition exists for a foreign legal entity to have both a representative office and to establish a

Table 2.10   Business Procedural Ranking – Ukraine

Ease of...	2006 rank	2005 rank	Change in rank
Doing business	128	132	+4
Starting a business	101	122	+21
Dealing with licenses	107	117	+10
Employing workers	107	109	+2
Registering property	133	134	+1
Getting credit	65	59	–6
Protecting investors	142	141	–1
Paying taxes	174	174	0
Trading across borders	106	98	–8
Enforcing contracts	26	26	0
Closing a business	139	135	–4

Source: The World Bank, <www.doingbusiness.org/ExploreEconomies>.

wholly owned subsidiary simultaneously. Joint ventures between Ukrainian and western partners became popular shortly after the county's transformation to a market economy. Ukrainian law sets no limitations on the formation of joint ventures

To register local offices of foreign companies in Ukraine, a $2,500 fee must be paid to the Ministry of Economy and European Integration of Ukraine in addition to all appropriate documentation. These documents must be submitted to the Ministry of Economy and European Integration of Ukraine no later than six months after issue in the country of origin, be legalized in the consular offices of Ukraine, presented in Ukrainian and translated by an official Ukrainian translator. Registration documents include: an application for registration printed on the firm's letterhead signed by its chief officer and sealed with the company seal; an extract from the Trade Register of the country of location of an officially registered central management body of a foreign business entity; a bank certificate of the financial institution including account number which services the company; and a warrant in the name of the individual who will execute representative functions for the company in Ukraine. Assuming that all required documents have been submitted, registration should occur within 60 days. Within one month of obtaining a registration certificate, a representative office must register with local Ukrainian tax inspectors.

Ukrainian companies typically prefer establishing long-term business relations on consignment. Foreign investors are urged to begin with small sales and advance full pre-payments. The Ukrainian "Law on Business Associations" was the only legal framework that regulated Ukrainian business associations until 2004. Since then, new codes have been issued which, in addition to the "Law on Business Associations," set the basic framework by which the most common forms of business entities are formed and operate.

LOCAL DISTRIBUTION NETWORKS

A competent distribution network is required in Ukraine as a result of the country's immense size and relatively high population dispersion. A local representative or distributor is advisable in light of the progress Ukraine has yet to make in terms of business transparency. Many trade hubs exists in Ukraine, and it is important to seek distributors that have the access to as many as possible, including Odessa, Lvov, Zaporizhzhya, Dnipropetrovsk, Donetsk, and Kharkiv – all important industrial centers with large populations. An important advantage to dealing with local agents and distributors is that they can help manage the complex task of acquiring certification and licenses for imported products. In addition, they can offer insight into local commercial intelligence for foreign investors, especially regarding new emerging markets. This is especially true as dependable information such as credit and background information is still greatly lacking on Ukrainian firms. Such is also the case for Ukrainian agents and distributors, which is why it is advisable to seek legal counsel or a market entry facilitator on all matters. Foreign exporters should also be aware of the numerous duties and commercial risks that will influence pricing, and adopt flexible and long-term presence operational policies.

MARKETING STRATEGIES

A growing number of Ukrainian customers admire western manufactured products such as cosmetics, automobiles, electronics and household appliances. However, Ukrainian consumers generally view products such as food and liquor from the West as being of poorer quality than those produced in Ukraine. Consumer conservatism, therefore, and a tendency to opt for familiar products, also play a major role in Ukrainian consumer behavior. Distribution warehouses, exhibitions, trade shows, and mailing catalogs are usually used to market industrial goods. Television advertising has also proven itself to be an efficient means of exposing Ukrainians to unfamiliar product names. Additionally, ingredient lists where relevant as well as warranties are respected by local consumers. For the most part, Ukrainian consumers tend to shy away from western brand names that are manufactured in Asia or some former socialist countries, with Belarus and Russia being exceptions. This is the case due to the existence of many counterfeit products under western names on the market; consumers have become wary of fake goods at artificially high prices.

A local address, therefore, can greatly increase consumer confidence.

Large department, specialty or chain stores generally serve as the means of marketing consumer goods; discount superstores do not exist at all. The introduction of low-cost retail superstore chains such as Wal-Mart may possibly reshape the local Ukrainian consumer goods market and increase its potential significantly.

Although franchising is not yet common in Ukraine, several firms have successfully made use of such a business strategy, and it remains a potentially successful way of doing business in Ukraine. McDonald's, Xerox, Kodak, Baskin Robbins, T.G.I. Friday's, Hertz, Pizza Hut, Celentano, the Potato House are some examples of successful franchise efforts in Ukraine. However, expensive bank loans, an undeveloped leasing system, and obscure IPR legislation remain barriers for franchises and small businesses alike.

Trade shows are also an important means of marketing products in Ukraine. Major local trade show organizers and fair authorities include: Medvin, PremierExpo, Euroindex, ACCO International, International Exhibition Center, and KievExpoPlaza.

PRICING

Prices in Ukraine generally remain relatively high due to high import tariffs, direct and indirect taxes, and a high VAT. Also, most Ukrainians tend to associate high prices with high quality, a fact that has been recognized and taken advantage of by some suppliers. Correlation between education level and product demand is not as evident as in other economies since many educated consumers remain part of the nation's low-income population. Price-setting authorities run by the Cabinet of Ministers of Ukraine regulate prices and tariffs according to changes in production and sale conditions.

LEGAL REVIEW

JUDICIARY

A civil law system exists in Ukraine which relies on codes and acts, while its court system consists of constitutional courts and general jurisdiction courts, including courts designated by specialization and by administrative level. These administrative levels are the Rayon, Oblast, and the Supreme Court – the highest court in the general courts system. All three courts handle civil, criminal, and administrative cases. Specialized arbitrage courts handle business disputes, bankruptcy, and anti-monopoly cases. The Constitutional Court interprets the Constitution and laws of Ukraine.

Ukraine's legal infrastructure remains weak, and it is therefore extremely important to acquire solid legal council both before and during commercial activity. Despite the fact that improvements have been made in Ukraine's rule of law, corporate governance regulations can make investment frustrating and difficult at times. Foreign investors express little confidence in the Ukrainian court system, which tends to strike down or ignore contractual provisions for international arbitration. Laws passed on the enforcement of foreign court decisions have not generally resulted in significant improvements. Moreover, investors often criticize Ukraine's legal system for burdensome procedures, unpredictability, political interference, corruption, and inefficiency. Even when they obtain favorable decisions, investors claim they are often not enforced. Therefore, most foreign investors in Ukraine consider the local and national court systems unpredictable and try to avoid them. Investment disputes that arise for such investors generally involve corruption, and relative lack of proper corporate governance or adequate law in Ukraine. Additionally, Ukrainian laws and regulations are vague, with considerable room for interpretation. As a result, many commercial contracts permit parties to use international arbitration courts to settle disputes.

The Washington Convention was ratified by Ukraine in 2000 enabling the International Center for Settlement of Investment Disputes (ICSID) to resolve investment disputes between investors and the Ukrainian government. Ukraine is a member of the New York Convention of 1958 on the Recognition and Enforcement of Foreign Arbitration Awards, while in 1994, Ukraine enacted an International Commercial Arbitration Law, paralleling commercial arbitration laws of the United Nations Commission on International Trade Law.

RIGHTS AND RESTRICTION FOR FOREIGN INVESTORS

Foreign investors and Ukrainian citizens are entitled to equal treatment under Ukraine's 1996 law "On Foreign Investment Regime." Some restrictions, however, apply in publishing and broadcasting. Foreigners are also prohibited from manufacturing weapons or alcoholic spirits. Private ownership by Ukrainian residents as well as foreign individuals and foreign legal entities is ensured among those entities able to own property under Ukrainian law, while owners may keep revenues and production derived from use of such land. Occasional difficulties, however, have arisen over foreign acquisition of majority control of enterprises.

Under Ukraine's Land Code, individuals cannot own more than a total of 100 hectares of agricultural land after 2008 and before 2015. A 20-year moratorium exists on agricultural land sales to foreigners, though foreigners are allowed to own land plots on which companies have been established. Despite such impediments, land leasing is an active Ukrainian market for both locals and foreigners. Ukraine strictly controls and restricts the import of certain pharmaceutical and communications related products, weapons, narcotics, chemical and hazardous substances. The relevant Ukrainian government ministry should be contacted if the above goods are to be imported. Qualified foreign investors are provided guarantees against nationalization under the "Foreign Investment Law" of 1996. However, in the case of national emergencies, accidents, or epidemics, the law may be circumvented.

Numerous permits are required by the Ukrainian government by companies to conduct business. Procedures for acquiring such permits are oftentimes complex, unpredictable, burdensome, and duplicative. As result, added cost and time is required to do business in Ukraine, which has in turn led to corruption and the development of shadow economy. "One-stop Registration Shops" have been introduced in several cities by municipal authorities in an attempt to alleviate the problem, while some cities have even begun to apply similar procedures and other permits such as land use.

Likewise, licensing fees are often high and procedures burdensome. Additionally, domestic producers and traders of ethyl, cognac, and fruit alcohol, spirits, and tobacco are favored under Ukraine's licensing laws. A Law "On Licensing Certain Types of Economic Activities" provides details on which activities are subject to licensing.

Foreign insurance companies must establish a registered commercial presence in Ukraine to invest in local companies, since insurance companies registered in Ukraine are the only companies allowed to carry out insurance operations. A lower minimum capital requirement exists for domestic insurance companies than insurance companies with foreign shareholders.

Foreign citizens bringing more than $10,000 in cash or $50,000 in checks into Ukraine must obtain a special license under Ukrainian law, while all cash must be declared upon entry into the country. The Multilateral Investment Guarantee Agency (MIGA) of the World Bank Group provides guarantees against political risk to foreign investors in connection with new investment in developing member countries. These investments include equity, loans, loan guarantees, and loans made by financial institutions, and certain non-equity direct investments.

INTELLECTUAL PROPERTY

Trademark piracy continues to be a common problem in Ukraine as copyrights laws still need to be amended and the country remains one of the major transit points for pirated material from Russia. Law enforcement may not be the best means of preventing piracy, as some state agencies have been known in the past to resell seized products. In addition, customs procedures for the registration of goods containing intellectual property can be a frustrating and burdensome experience.

Nonetheless, support for copyright amendments in Ukraine is growing, while it has become a signatory to a number of international agreements and conventions and is a member of the World International Property Organization. In addition, numerous new laws have been passed to improve the protection of intellectual property. Ukraine has made significant efforts to bring its legislation in line with the Trade-Related Aspects of Intellectual Property Rights (TRIPS) requirements for WTO membership, and has passed a law to bring all regulations into compliance with TRIPS. As a result, authorities have begun making progress in stopping the manufacture of illegal products.

STANDARDIZATION AND CERTIFICATION

Despite the fact that Ukraine is working towards harmonizing its standardization and certification system with international norms, current procedures can be lengthy, burdensome, and expensive. Standards are vague, inflexible, and subject to frequent change. Several certification bodies operate independently without coordination or oversight. Additionally, local, regional, and municipal authorities often require additional documentation beyond that required by certification bodies. Conformity assessment to ensure consistency during all stages of the production process is mandatory for all manufacturers under Ukrainian law. Appropriate resources, however, such as modern analytical equipment and reactants, are not available in most testing laboratories.

The country is striving to bring its standardization system into conformity with the European Standards System by 2011, and Ukraine now belongs to several international standardization bodies, including the International Organization for Standardization (ISO). The Ukrainian National Accreditation Body was established to ensure the use of standards and procedures consistent with the European Cooperation for Accreditation policy. Despite this, Ukrainian authorities generally do not recognize foreign product certificates, even if they are in line with international standards.

Separate regulation exists for accreditation and certification. Importers can apply for a certificate for a single batch of goods: a one-year certificate for all imported goods during that year, and a 5-year certificate that mandates inspection of production facilities. Conformity certificates may be either a Certificate of Acceptance of a foreign certification issued by the State Committee of Ukraine on Technical Regulation and Consumer Policy or a

Conformance Certificate issued by a Ukrainian agency upon certification of goods. Certification and approval can at times be lengthy, duplicative, and expensive. However, some Ukrainian certification bodies can evaluate the quality of a production system rather than the quality of a single product. However, with this certificate, only selective goods will be certified.

BUSINESS ETHICS

According to the Institute of the Central-European Political Studies, Ukrainian authorities plan to introduce special anti-corruption criteria throughout all levels of governmental decision-making. These include legislative drafts with respect the to distribution and control of social spending, with special attention being paid to property rights and intellectual property. However, until such measures can be implemented efficiently, foreign investors are strongly urged to acquire local representatives and distributors in Ukraine as transparency in business transactions is still lacking.

In addition, it is highly advisable to seek legal counsel both prior to and throughout the duration of doing business in Ukraine. It is also advisable to consider including an anti-bribery provision when drafting a contract with a Ukrainian company, as well acquiring a lawyer, accountant, interpreter or private investor fluent in Ukrainian or Russian.

Ukrainian statistics are often unreliable, and "experts" can easily be swayed by conflicts of interest. Furthermore, banks do not provide information on the financial status of clients, nor is there a nationwide service for registering enterprises of doubtful solvency. Many suppliers of dubious origin continue to operate in Ukraine's market, and exporters should be aware that money laundering operations exist amongst many local competitors selling so-called quality goods.

INVESTMENT OPPORTUNITIES

CONSTRUCTION AND REGENERATION

Ukraine's developing construction industry has an estimated annual building material market valued at some $570–580 million. This competitive industry is constantly seeking new supply sources and contacts. Many European distributors have already begun aggressively promoting their products; some distributors have established joint ventures to manufacture building materials in Ukraine. Industrial regions may offer opportunities for cooperating with importers, while prices for such products are generally higher in remote areas of the country. Low-cost items are generally provided for by local producers.

The following items are especially desirable in Ukraine's construction market: acrylic paints, insulation, carpeting, linoleum and interior ceramic tiles. However, local manufacturers generally import chemical binding, conditioning, and coupling agents since locally produced versions are usually of low quality. Opportunities for importing such goods, however, have been growing. Cement, bricks, clay roofing and asphalt shingles are in low demand, while metal roofing components are in moderate demand.

PHARMACEUTICALS AND MEDICAL EQUIPMENT

In recent years Ukraine's pharmaceutical market has demonstrated stable growth as a result of a rise in imports as well as local production. Most multinational pharmaceutical manufacturers have representative offices or operate in Ukraine through local distributors, while around 60 major pharmaceutical manufacturers in the country export primarily to Russia and the CIS countries. Some multinationals may look closely at potential acquisitions or joint ventures in Ukraine. Domestic pharmaceutical manufacturers generally supply generic drugs and vitamins, and operate in the lowest price range of the market. Firms which sell large volumes of over the counter drugs generally have the best sales performance. The best selling anatomical and therapeutic pharmaceuticals include analgesics, antibiotics, vitamins, cough & cold preparations, cholagogue-hepatics, phycoleptics and vasotherapeuticals.

Medical equipment in the Ukraine is mainly imported, with Germany being the largest supplier. Local medical equipment traders have extensive networks and the ability to identify buyers and can therefore be extremely helpful for the investor. Market potential for laboratory equipment, diagnostic systems and disposable items, electro-medical equipment, dental equipment, radiographic units, and laser surgery devices are in high demand, in addition to high-quality, advanced diagnostic and therapeutic equipment. Modern equipment is also in need for microsurgery, radiology and biomedicine, while popularity is rising for laser-optics in vascular surgery, gastroenterology, dermatology and neurosurgery.

AGRICULTURE AND AGRICULTURAL MACHINERY

Nearly 97 percent of foodstuffs consumed in Ukraine are produced locally, including meat, poultry and dairy products; as well as macaroni, confectionery and bakery products, alcohol and non-alcoholic drinks, canned meat and vegetables. However, domestic production and consumption of agricultural products is only about half of what they were during the last years of the Soviet era. A number of consumer-oriented products for export potential to Ukraine have been identified by the Foreign Agricultural Service in Kiev (FAS/Kiev). These include livestock genetics and seeds for planting, wine, pork, high-quality beef, seafood, pet food and snack food.

Ukraine requires an annual supply of some $1–2 billion worth of farm equipment. Furthermore, the demand to replenish physically depreciated farm and processing equipment is estimated at some $5–10 billion, with nearly 70 to 80 percent of such machinery requiring replacement or replenishment; almost half of all tractors are 15–25 years old. Demand for used machinery is also in demand, as the supply of such machinery has decreased. Most agricultural machinery such as ploughs, harrows, cultivators, seeders and sprayers are provided by one of the country's manufacturers, who number around 40 presently. Only about 15 to 30 percent of production facilities of most agricultural machinery plants are currently being utilized. As a result, domestically produced agricultural machinery can be relatively expensive, as inefficient and outdated technology continues to be used. Ukrainians generally trust foreign agricultural machinery, as some firms have already entered the market and have a good reputation. Good investment opportunities remain for foreign companies to enter the Ukrainian agricultural machinery market. Additionally, the acquisition of modern farm products in Ukraine would also have a substantial effect on the nation's agricultural productivity in general.

PESTICIDES

The agricultural chemicals market offers many opportunities for producers as Ukraine's pesticide market remains substantial. An estimated 30 percent of harvested crops are lost due to problems that could be alleviated by pesticides. About 70–80 percent of Ukrainian pesticides are imported. Most companies currently marketing pesticides in Ukraine represent European subsidiaries of multinational firms. There are around thirty firms marketing agricultural chemicals in Ukraine currently. Weed, plant disease and insect combatants are considered promising investment opportunities for agricultural chemical suppliers in Ukraine.

FOOD PROCESSING AND PACKAGING EQUIPMENT

Food processing is one of the fastest-developing sectors of Ukraine's economy, growing some 30 percent annually. In 2004, 15 percent of Ukraine's total direct foreign investment came from investments into Ukraine's food industry, which amounted to some $988.3 million. The need for food processing and packaging machinery continues to rise steadily as the nation's food industry is quickly transformed into a relatively developed market with both international and local brands. Nearly 97 percent of foodstuffs consumed in Ukraine are produced domestically. Furthermore, Ukraine also has the potential of becoming an important exporter of processed food to the former Soviet Republics, Central Europe, and the Black Sea Basin. Coupled with the expanding industry, in many cases no local manufacturers exist for certain food-processing and packaging equipment. Equipment for higher value-added processing or secondary processing, energy-efficient equipment, small-capacity production equipment and packaging equipment that ensures a longer shelf-life are in growing demand.

AIRPORT EQUIPMENT AND SERVICES

Ukrainian civil aviation traffic has increased from 6 percent annually in 2000 to some 36.4 percent in 2004, while air cargo transportation grew by over 64.3 percent in 2003. Experts believe that the upward trend in civil aviation will continue in Ukraine, especially as the market was unaffected by the global slowdown in aviation after the September 11 attacks on the United States. Some six million passengers annually can be serviced by Ukraine's airports, though currently airports operate at only 40 percent of their full capacity and are based on technology of the 1990s. Ukraine's largest airport is the Kyiv-Boryspil (KBP), servicing over 50 percent of the country's commercial air traffic. The Ukrainian government would like to turn KBP into a Central and Eastern European hub for major international connections.

Almost all of Ukraine's regional airports are in need of modernization and investment in such areas as communication, transport, runways, passenger and cargo terminals, and other needs of airport infrastructure including lighting, elevators, loading containers, heating and cooling systems, as well as security systems. Today, few local manufacturers exist for such requirements, save for steel structure fabrication and construction. In addition, air navigation equipment is also in need of modernization, while new air traffic control centers are also required. Other opportunities exist in conversion projects of former military airbases into cargo airports. Interested investors should establish long-term partnerships directly with the Ukrainian civil aviation authority and Ukrainian airports. Foreign investors have a competitive advantage in software system investments, as well as engineering, consultant, management services.

SECURITY AND SAFETY EQUIPMENT

Domestic manufacturers are unable to meet demands for Ukraine's security and safety equipment thereby making this market an attractive one for foreign investors. This is especially true of high-tech end of security products, with many citizens relying on security devices for their homes and cars. Additionally, a growing number of private banks and corporations require security software, safety deposit boxes, safes, metal detectors, pagers, smoke detectors, and sophisticated turn-key security and access control systems. High-tech antiterrorist equipment is also in demand. Trade exhibition can be extremely helpful in foreign contacts for this market.

AUTOMOTIVE PARTS

More than 200,000 cars were purchased in 2004 by Ukrainians at an estimated value of $1.5 billion, while more than 5.5 million cars were registered in the country during the same year. A 2–3 percent annual increase in the number of cars in possession is expected to continue or grow. Most cars in the country have an engine volume of less than 2,000 cubic centimeters. Auto part sales is a highly competitive industry in Ukraine for both western and non-western car models, with new and used spare part sales valued at some $240 million annually. Spare parts account for around $70 million of the total automotive car market in Ukraine.

The Ukrainian market for car body, engine, fuel and electric car parts is estimated at $30 million annually, with parts most vulnerable to accidents such as lights, bumpers, radiator grills, etc. being in highest demand. Additionally, the following products and services comprise a large part of the auto parts market in Ukraine: some 1.1 million car batteries are sold yearly, around 20 percent of which, totaling $14 million, are imported; 25 percent of Ukraine's $30 million-a-year air and gas filter industry is supplied from non-CIS countries; tire sales amount to some $80–85 million annually, around half of which are imported; automotive glass sales are estimated at $15 million yearly, $10 million of which is from imports; anti-theft security devices are estimated at $12–15 million annually; automobile brakes and parts potential is valued at $20–23 million annually; and shock absorbers account for an estimated $15 million of the annual car parts market, with imports accounting for 70 percent.

COMPUTER SOFTWARE, SERVICES AND ACCESSORIES

Enforcement of intellectual property regulations combined with the strengthening of Ukraine's economy has increased demand for computer software for industrial and business needs while a more transparent market for computer software is arising. Sales leaders in the software market are generally accounting programs, operating systems, office applications, archives and antivirus packages.

Around 98 percent of all computers have Windows and Microsoft's Office programs installed on them, with some 90 percent being illegal. Illegal imports have had a marked influence on the size of Ukraine's software market. Despite such circumstances, foreign software suppliers reported sales growth rates of some 24–53 percent in 2004, especially for security software, and nearly one million personal computers are known to have been sold in 2004 according to industry sources, more than 90 percent of which are assembled in the Ukraine. International brands, however, account for some 70 percent of laptop computers; experts expect these systems to increase rapidly in popularity and market share. Computer manufacturers represent less than 10 percent of computer companies. Government procurement accounts for 65 percent of the total computer market. Systems integration, software, maintenance and repair offer far more lucrative opportunities than do hardware sales, however. Computer components for Ukrainian assemblers are mainly derived from Asia, while Europe supplies computer peripherals.

Computer software services are also growing in desirability, while some 25,000 certified programmers are employed in the Ukrainian industry, making the county an important low cost site for high quality software development. Experts agree that software exports grow better than the domestic market, with export sales of software between $70 million and $200 million, while average annual export sales for forty leading software-developing firms vary from $315,000 to $6 million per company.

IT AND TELECOMMUNICATIONS

Significant changes have occurred over the past decade in Ukraine's telecommunications and IT industry, particularly in mobile wireless and internet. The average level of teledensity is more than 25 percent, while revenues from long distance and international calls account for almost a third of total services provided by the industry. The nation's telecom industry, it should be noted, falls behind the rest of the national economy in its movement toward liberalization, transparency and openness for foreign investments. Additionally, internet services are one of the leading sub-sectors of the Ukrainian telecom industry, with around 6 million internet users in the country.

POWER GENERATION

Nuclear and thermal coal/gas-fired power plants supply most of Ukraine's power. The government owns the country's nuclear sub sector while Russia continues to supply all nuclear fuel and essential equipment to Ukraine. More than $90 million per year is spent to ship Ukraine's spent nuclear fuel to Russia for storage. The first dry storage for spent nuclear fuel was put into operation at the Zaporizka Nuclear Power Plant in 2001 under the management of American Duke Engineering. Plans to construct a central spent fuel storage facility at the Chernobyl site for Ukraine's 15 operating nuclear reactors by the government are ongoing. In January 2005, the US Holtec International won the tender to build this facility. These reactors provide around half of the entire county's electricity. High-voltage and energy-saving technologies, accumulator batteries, assorted bearings, circuit breakers, disconnectors, support insulators, and generating sets are in high demand. In addition, power distribution technology, equipment and software are also required as well as equipment for thermal power plants. Renewable power technology is also in demand.

GAS AND OIL FIELD MACHINERY

Ukraine's hydrocarbon resources are estimated at 7–8 billion tons of fuel equivalent, while the average annual oil and gas production amounts to 18 billion cubic meters of natural gas, covering some 21–24 percent of domestic demand, and 4 million tons of crude oil, meeting 10–12 percent of local need. Pumping equipment capable of producing below 6,000 feet is in need as it is not manufactured in Ukraine despite the fact that fields on-shore are at depths of 10,000 to 15,000 feet. Much drilling equipment has difficulty drilling below 15,000 feet. Ukrainian production of drilling machinery and stimulation technologies is also limited. Although substantial offshore natural gas and crude oil reserves exist, Ukraine does not have the technology to drill underwater deeper than 70–80 meters (200 feet). Additionally, even though Ukraine has the second largest refinery capacity in the CIS, utilization still stands at less than half. A host of equipment is needed for Ukraine's gas and oil field industry, including: oil and gas exploration equipment, drilling technology for offshore projects deeper than 200 feet underwater, technologies for gas production, storage and transport, pipeline leak control systems as well as fittings and applications, welding machines, cranes, monitoring and control systems for gas and oil pipelines, fuel storage tanks and desulphurization and quality control facilities to name only a few. In addition, refineries rehabilitation & upgrade, crude oil and gas transit and distribution, as well as Coal Bed Methane (CBM) development, are also in high demand.

ENVIRONMENTAL GOODS AND SERVICES

Ukraine is preparing for a new environmental policy in line with the international process "Environment for Europe" leading to the proposal of a number of projects including waste treatment in the coal mining and construction industries. In addition, thermal power and oil refining modernization and soil remediation are also important.

Safety improvements at industrial and municipal plants, water conservation projects and improvement of filtration efficiency are considered potentially lucrative areas for investment despite the fact that the market for waste recycling equipment is only in the development phase. Reuse of coal waste and steel slag for construction materials and a general rise in the proportion of recycled materials is a positive sign. Industrial enterprises are also in need of new water and air pollution control systems.

LEISURE AND TOURISM

Despite problems of lack of capital and transparency, tourism has become one of the key drivers of the Ukrainian economy. In Crimea alone, tourism revenue comprises more than half of the government budget annually. A growing middle-class population along with rising income levels spell potential for this industry. Thousands of dollars are spent by Ukrainians in such areas as Southeast Asia, Bali, Seychelles, South Africa and Kenya. Good investment opportunities are also available for tourism infrastructure development. Hotel, resort and theme park development, winter sports facilities and convention business are some promising options in this industry as well.

RETAIL

Over the past several years, retail turnover has surpassed Ukraine's GDP growth, making this sector one of the nation's most promising, as market experts believe the actual size of the retail market in Ukraine is between $50 and $75 billion. Small and medium-sized traditional stores, open-air markets, and kiosks still dominate the market currently. However, large multi-functional shopping centers are beginning to take hold. In 2005, almost half of all retail space in Kiev was offered in large outlets, while international commercial property management consultant Colliers International estimates that the demand for retail space will continue to exceed the supply for the next several years. Some commentators estimate the market volume of large retail centers to be somewhere between $400 and $600 million. The return on investment index for the large retail centers in Kiev is one of the best in Eastern Europe, varying from three to five years.

PUBLIC PROCUREMENT

Foreign investors have additional opportunities with large government procurements. However, Ukraine is not yet a signatory of the WTO Agreement on Government Procurement. Procurement of government goods and services valued above EUR 40,000 must be conducted via tenders. Companies should track the tender announcements of western tender vendors, the World Bank and the European Bank for Reconstruction and Development (EBRD) for such ventures.

GENERAL INFORMATION

LANGUAGE

Since 1990, Ukrainian has been the official state language of Ukraine. Russian is also understood by most, while younger Ukrainians are considerably more familiar with English than older generations.

LOCAL CUSTOMS

The legacy of centralized authority which has existed in Ukraine for hundreds of years makes it difficult to generalize about customs for engaging in western-style business which most Ukrainians know little about. Oftentimes, duplicate forms which include signatures, proper letterhead, and stamps of authenticity are required for business transactions.

The form of business may be more important to a Ukrainian business partner than substance, making a foreign partner's approach extremely important. It can sometimes be helpful to take an educational role in business negotiations, while being responsive to one's negotiating partner, even regarding seemingly inconsequential matters. A strong emphasis is placed on cementing personal relationships before doing business, while in-person meetings are essential, with little business conducted over the phone. Business cards, firm handshakes, social outings and remembering your partner's birthday, child's birthday, and Ukrainian holidays will be very helpful and appreciated.

In 2005 a rise in the number of physical attacks against foreigners was reported. These incidents, however, were all isolated and there is generally little opposition to foreign business people in particular.

VISAS

Visas are not issued at the point of entry into Ukraine, and anyone without a valid entry visa arriving at any point of entry will be denied entry and turned back at their own expense.

TRANSPORTATION

Private taxis can also be hired for a reasonable price by phone, though trains are considerably cheaper and fairly reliable, albeit slow and less convenient. Air travel within Ukraine is generally unreliable, with unpredictable schedules.

HELPFUL RESOURCES – UKRAINE

GOVERNMENT RESOURCES

Ministry of Economy of Ukraine: www.me.gov.ua/
State Customs Service of Ukraine: www.customs.gov.ua/
The National Bank of Ukraine: www.bank.gov.ua
State Customs Service: www.customs.gov.ua
Ministry of Labor and Social Policy: www.mlsp.kiev.ua
Statistics Committee of Ukraine: http://www.ukrstat.gov.ua
Ministry of Economy and European Integration of Ukraine:
http://zakon.rada.gov.ua/cgi-bin/laws/main.cgi
http://zakon.rada.gov.ua/
Ministry of Internal Affairs: www.centrmia.gov.ua
Ministry of Economy and European Integration: www.me.gov.ua
Ministry of Industrial Policy of Ukraine: www.industry.gov.ua
State Commission on Securities and Stocks: www.ssmsc.gov.ua
State Customs Service of Ukraine: www.customs.gov.ua/
State Department of Intellectual Property: www.spou.kiev.ua/
State Committee of Ukraine for Technical Regulation and Consumer Policy: www.dssu.gov.ua/
www.dssu.gov.ua/control/en/index
Conformity Assessment Bodies: www.dssu.gov.ua/sertif/perelik.html
Law of Ukraine on Conformity Assessment: www.welcometo.kiev.ua
Ministry of Health of Ukraine: www.moz.gov.ua
Ministry of Agrarian Policy:
        www.minagro.kiev.ua/newenglish/index.html
Ministry of Agrarian Policy:
        www.minagro.kiev.ua/newenglish/index.html

State Civil Aviation Authority: www.ukraviatrans.gov.ua
State Security Service of Ukraine: www.sbu.gov.ua/eng/
Ministry of Interior of Ukraine: www.kmu.gov.ua/control/en
State Foodstuffs Department of the Ministry of Agrarian Policy of
Ukraine: www.fooddept.gov.ua
State Department for Communications and Informatization of the
    Ministry of Transport of Ukraine: www.stc.gov.ua
Ministry of Economy & EI: www.me.gov.ua.
Ministry for Environmental Protection of Ukraine: www.menr.gov.ua
Ukrainian State Tourism Administration: www.tourism.gov.ua
Government of Ukraine:
www.kmu.gov.ua/control/en
www.president.gov.ua/eng/

TRADE SHOWS

Medvin Trade Show: www.medvin.kiev.ua
PremierExpo Trade Show: www.pe.com.ua
Euroindex Trade Show: www.euroindex.com.ua
ACCO International Trade Show: www.acco.com.ua
International Exhibition Center Trade Show: www.iec-expo.com.ua
KievExpoPlaza Trade Show: www.expoplaza.kiev.ua
Ukraine Travel Market Trade Show:
    www.autoexpo.com.ua/eng/ukraine.html
MaRHo Trade Show in the retail equipment:
    marho.euroindex.ua/indexe.php3
Euro index, leading organizer of IT trade shows in Ukraine:
    www.euroindex.com

MISCELLANEOUS

European Business Association Agrochemical Committee
http://eba.com.ua/activities/committees/agrochemical/
Agribusiness news: www.agriukraine.com, www.agroperspectiva.com/en
Aerosvit Ukrainian Airlines: http://www.aerosvit.com
Kyiv-Boryspil International Airport (KBP): www.airport-
    borispol.kiev.ua
Association IT Ukraine: www.itukraine.org.ua
Ukrainian Association of Software Developers: www.uaswd.org.ua
Leading IT publications and catalogs: www.itcpublishing.com/ua
Association of Computer Clubs: www.uacc.org.ua/en

Leading IT publications and catalogs: www.itcpublishing.com
Telecom Club: www.telecom-club.org.ua
UITT (International Travel & Tourism Trade Show): www.uitt-kiev.com
Ukrainian Association of Retail Centers: www.ua-retail.com
Colliers International in Ukraine: www.colliers.com/Markets/Ukraine/
Web-search engine for Ukraine: http://meta-ukraine.com/en/
http://www.bizukraine.com/employment.htm
http://ukraine-today.com/business/person_agenc/personnel_agencies.htm
http://ukraine-today.com/business/employment/index.shtml
www.ukrjob.hut.ru/agency.php
http://price.com.ua/
http://shop.bigmir.net/
http://itc.ua/hl/

Chapter 3

Investing in Latvia

LATVIA IS A STABLE DEMOCRACY WHICH boasts of having established a secure macroeconomic environment, rapid economic growth, a well-educated and easily adaptable workforce, and significant cost efficiencies. It lies at an important strategic location at the center of the three Baltic States, serving as a potential commercial, financial and transportation hub for the Nordic/Baltic region and access to some 600 million customers. With an economy based on service industries such as transportation, financial services and light industry such as wood, textiles and food processing, Latvia offers a friendly, English-speaking business environment to foreign investors. Latvian authorities impose little controls on imports and exports or on use and conversion of foreign currencies. Modern laws have been adopted by the Latvian governments including the establishment of copyrights, patents and trademarks which are supportive of starting businesses. Increasingly modernized telecommunication services, modern housing opportunities, and reasonably priced business venues make the country an attractive destination for investments. Furthermore, Latvia has a potentially lucrative market for foreign IT equipment and services, capital machinery and equipment, and consumer products.

In recent years, the government also made significant efforts to increase efficiency of revenue collection in order to lessen internal government deficits. Although a large portion of significant enterprises remain in the hands of the Latvian government, most banks, companies, and real estate have been privatized. In 1999 Latvia joined the World Trade Organization, and in 2004 it became a member of the EU and of NATO. Since then, Latvia has proven to be a stable democracy making impressive strides through continuous political and economic reforms towards a market economy. With EU accession, Latvia participates in EMU and hopes to become part of the EU monetary zone in 2008.

Latvia recently marked its 15-year anniversary of independence and free market reform. With sound macroeconomic fundamentals, a highly successful monetary policy, and a commitment to fiscal conservatism, the country has transformed itself into an attractive investment environment with potentially lucrative opportunities. Both unemployment and inflation continue to decline, while Latvia's foreign debt remains a relatively low percentage of its GDP. Meanwhile, foreign reserves of the Bank of Latvia continue to guarantee the stability of the Latvian national currency, the lat (LS), while EU membership and Free Trade treaties with the CIS makes Latvia an ideal place to do business.

Although a member of the EU since 2004, Latvia continues to use the Lat, as it has yet to complete all stages of the Economic Monetary Union. The plural of a lat (ISO code LVL) is 'lati', or 'latu'. One LS is equivalent to approximately 1.89 USD.

POLITICAL BACKGROUND

POLITICAL STRUCTURE

The Latvian government is a Parliamentary Democracy and has a constitution, or Satversme, adopted in 1922 and re-adopted on December 10, 1991. Latvia's cabinet of Council of Ministers is nominated by the prime minister and appointed by the unicameral Parliament or Saeima. The Saeima has 100 seats, whose members are elected by direct, popular vote to serve four-year terms.

Under the Latvian constitution the Saeima approves all Latvian laws and is responsible for making strategic decisions on political and economic development of the Latvian state.

Latvia has had eleven governments since independence, none of which has served out a full parliamentary term as a result of the fragmentation of the nation's political make-up. Such instability, however, has had limited impact on broad policy consensus, while an open economy and pro-Western foreign policy continues to be favored. Additionally, all transfers of power have been orderly while political institutions created as part of parliamentary democracy generally function smoothly and garner wide public support. Despite Latvia's fractious and short-lived governments, political stability risk is low, and the impact of such a situation has relatively little impact on economic policy or business operations for foreign investors.

Key Figures

Latvia's president and chief of state since 1999 is President Vaira Vike-Freibderga, while the head of government is Prime Minister Aigars Kalvitis since December 2004. The president is reelected by Parliament for a four-year term, while the president appoints the prime minister.

Political Developments and Foreign Relations

In 1940, Latvia was annexed by the Soviet Union after a period of independence between World War I and Word War II. Following the disintegration of the USSR, Latvia regained its independence in 1991, though Russian troops remained on Latvian soil until as late as 1994. The 1997 Latvian–Russian boundary treaty remains unsigned, as Russia has set the improved treatment of Latvia's Russian minority as a pre-condition to the treaty's ratification, while Latvians demand that Russia agree to a declaration that admits Soviet aggression during the World War II. A 1998 maritime boundary treaty between Latvia and Lithuania has also yet to be ratified, due mainly to issues concerning oil exploration rights. Today, nearly one-third of Latvia's modest population of some 2.3 million is Russian, causing Moscow some concern. Although Latvia's relations with its Russian neighbor remain strained as a result of Latvia's significant Russian ethnic minority, the unsigned Latvian – Russian border treaty, and unresolved historical questions relating to the Soviet Union's occupation of Latvia between 1945 and 1991, the country has taken important steps towards integrating its Russian minority and dealing with such issues, and almost no risk of conflict exists with Latvia and its neighbors.

Latvia has also concluded bilateral investment agreements with the majority of European and CEE countries and the United States, some of which are being renegotiated to meet EU requirements. In the spring of 2004, Latvia joined both NATO and the EU, which protects the country from undue Russian pressure. Currently, Latvia is contributing troops to the US-led stabilization force in Iraq, so that though the risk of a terrorist attack is low, it is not entirely absent.

ECONOMIC REVIEW

BACKGROUND AND PROJECTIONS

Latvia is an upper middle-income country with a population of 2.3 million, more than one-third of whom lives in the capital city of Riga. With some 40 percent of the country covered in forests, Latvia imports all of its natural gas and oil, as well as part of its electricity, having little natural resources of its own other than timber. With labor shortages and inflationary pressures mounting, Latvia stands at a crossroads in terms of its economy, which has made remarkable strides since the mid-1990s. Traditionally the poorest economy based on GDP per capita in the region, in recent years it has been expanding ahead of potential due to strong growth in the retail, construction, real estate and telecommunication sectors. The nation's economy continued to surge in 2006, with gross domestic product growth peaking at 11.9 percent. Although the achievement was probably the best in the EU as Latvia's economy rides the wave of an EU integration-related boom, its consequences have given rise to real, external, and financial vulnerabilities. The new Latvian government, which appears overly optimistic about potential risks to the nation's economy, will need to sustain growth and maintain macroeconomic stability by moderating the pace of growth. Although in general Latvia's economic development is a success story, rapid growth has also led to growing imbalances, and the risks are increasing of a downturn. Private and public demand has pushed the economy beyond its supply capacity, while domestic drivers of inflation are becoming entrenched. Inflation continues to run rampant, with recent figures showing that in January 2007 Latvia's rates was one of the highest in the EU, amounting to more than 7 percent. Furthermore, the current account deficit has failed to moderate, adding to the economy's already high external debt burden.

Although Latvia's relative per capita income in purchasing power (PPP) terms remains the lowest in the EU at 43 points, it has nonetheless climbed 16 percentage points, a fact reflected in strong growth in factor productivity, as well as by rapid investment and expansion of employment. Moody's, Standard & Poor's and Fitch IBCA (2005) established that Latvia is considered a stable environment for investment in terms of its credit ratings. Despite the fact that Latvia's economy was hard-hit by the 1998 Russian economic crisis as more than one-third of its exports were to the CIS area, the event did not significantly affect Latvia's rating, and credit agencies noted that political and economic stability of Latvia is today equal or better than neighboring Central European countries. Following the crisis, strict government regulations were implemented including a reorientation of Latvian exports away from Russia and towards the EU and implementation of budget cuts recommended by IMF. As a result, trade and FDI figures began to improve and Latvia's economy began to slowly pick up. Steering the economy towards stability and away from its overheated path is now a major goal in order to maintain its good standing, which is made all the more difficult by the lack of effective monetary policy tools and by the excessively optimistic expectations by investors. Data from 2006 has reinforced concerns that the Latvian economy may be overheating. Economic growth has not slowed, reaching 11.8 percent year-on-year in the third quarter of 2006, while real GDP growth was up from 11.1 percent in the second quarter and kept growth close to 12 percent for the first three quarters of the year.

Latvia appears the most economically vulnerable of the three Baltic states, as some other economies have peaked while others have advanced at a more suitable pace. Dangerous imbalances have developed including a wide current-account deficit reaching 24.2 percent of GDP in the third quarter of 2006, up from 12.9 percent in the same period during the previous year, reaching 19.3 percent of GDP in the first nine months of 2006. Meanwhile, the economy is running a large positive output gap. Such growth has mainly been driven by a rapid expansion of domestic demand, fuelled by fast growth of banking credit. Lending to households was up by 80 percent year on year by the end of September 2006, and a housing price bubble may have developed, as house prices continue to rise by about 2 percent month on month. During the first six months of 2006 Latvia's economic activity gained momentum and the GDP growth reached 12.0 percent. Domestic demand simultaneously grew while export growth subsided. Investment growth, on the other hand, was strong, while the contribution of overall consumption to domestic demand also increased. The service sector rose faster than any other, with the annual growth in gross value added rising 8 percent. Trade and real estate, renting and business activities recorded development of some 18 percent. Progress in construction, which stood at 16.7 percent, drove expansion of Latvia's goods sector. Gross value added in manufacturing, on the other hand, grew by only 6.5 percent.

However, despite the fact that overheating is a prime concern, there is also a need to focus on allowing Latvia's export performance to remain

Table 3.1   Economic Indicators, 2006

Current GDP (US$ billion)	35.8
Real GDP growth rate (percent)	9.6
GDP per capita (PPP – US$)	15,400
Economic growth (yoy percent)	11.8
Current account deficit (percent of GDP)	15.7
Current account balance (US$ billion)	–2.538
Inflation rate (consumer prices) %	6.3
Investment (gross fixed) % of GDP	31.4
Public debt (% of GDP)	11
External debt (US$ billion)	18.9
Economic aid recipient (US$ million)	96.2

Source: World Factbook, 2006 – <Latvia http://www.cia.gov/cia/>.

favorable so that the country's external liabilities will be serviced. Higher interest rates have also dampened domestic demand somewhat, though the income gains of the "working for families" package have offset such effects somewhat. Increased business investment will ease capacity constraints and lead to greater productivity growth as well as real wages. A vigorous expansion in government consumption will also boost demand. Rising incomes and running savings and borrowings from banks that offer very low interest rates due to a larger inflow of foreign and EU money have in turn boosted consumption, on the other hand. Consumer price inflation remained at an estimated annual average of 6.5 percent in 2006, and a wage-price spiral may be developing. Real wage growth exceeded productivity increases, which averaged around 8 percent in the first half of 2006, standing at more than 15 percent year on year in the third quarter of 2006.

Annual consumer price inflation was sustained at a relatively high 6.7 percent during the first half of the year as a result of an increase in indirect taxes, strong consumer demand and high energy prices. The account deficit during the same period also rose to reach 17.6 percent of the GDP, mainly reflecting the increase in trade deficit. Also, as a result of shrinking wood and mineral product exports, export growth slowed to 14.5 percent while imports strengthened by 29.3 percent. The significant increase in tax collections, and of lower than expected budget expenditures, resulted in the general government budget posting a financial surplus of 4.2 percent of the GDP during the first half of 2006.

BUSINESS ENVIRONMENT

OVERVIEW

Hoping to attract further foreign direct investment and interest by foreign investors, Latvian authorities are actively working with investors to improve the country's business climate. Little screening of foreign investments exists apart from guidelines and regulations stipulated by the EU and WTO. One of the major strategic national goals of Latvian authorities is to accelerate integration into Euro-Atlantic organizations as well as the global economy. The government has thus worked to bring Latvian economic institutions, laws and regulations into conformity with EU directives. Broad changes were made to Latvia's legislation prior to its accession to the WTO in 1999, including instituting investment laws which apply equally to domestic and foreign investors.

Although changes made in 1996 to investment laws removed nearly all restrictions on foreign investment, impediments to trade and investment in Latvia continue to exist. These include the existence or perception of corruption, organized crime, and government bureaucracy typical of the old Soviet Bloc countries. However, many foreign companies still maintain that the county's business environment is among the best in the region, as the Latvian legal system and tax structures are moving closer to those in the industrialized west. The Latvian government has developed a good working relationship with the foreign business community via the Latvian Foreign Investors Council in order to streamline various bureaucratic procedures and to address legal and regulatory issues. Foreign investors in Latvia are extended national treatment by the Latvian government; therefore, most investment incentives and requirements apply equally to local and foreign businesses. Due to historical trade relations, companies from Norway, Sweden, Germany and Finland approach the Latvian market with great confidence.

In 1995, the Riga Stock Exchange (RSE) began operations with the help of France, which helped Latvia set up the securities market based on a continental European model. In 1997, the RSE was admitted to the International Federation of Stock Exchanges as a corresponding emerging market; it was the first exchange in Eastern Europe to create an index in cooperation with Dow Jones.

To sustain its present growth and competitiveness, new technologies are crucial since the country inherited an obsolete industrial base. In addition, IT equipment including telecommunications, electronic components and electrical machinery, are in growing demand. Latvia's rich supply of timber and generally outdated woodworking equipment result in the need for wood and forestry machinery supplies to be replaced or updated to meet the industry's full potential.

Table 3.2   Business Procedural Ranking – Latvia

Ease of doing business (out of a total of 175)	2005 rank	2006 rank	Change in rank
Doing business	31	24	+7
Starting a business	26	25	+1
Dealing with licenses	65	65	0
Employing workers	125	123	+2
Registering property	102	82	+20
Getting credit	19	13	+6
Protecting investors	43	46	–3
Paying taxes	106	52	+54
Trading across borders	27	28	–1
Enforcing contracts	11	11	0

Source: The World Bank, 2006 – <Latvia www.doingbusiness.org>.

Many sources of financing exist for investors interested in doing business with Latvia. These include the World Bank's International Finance Corporation, which provides financing options with a focus on developing infrastructure, health, education, financial services, agriculture, telecommunication and tourism; the European Bank for Reconstruction and Development for the areas of infrastructure, environment, industry and financial services; and the European Investment Bank for investments in infrastructure, telecommunications, energy, industry, environmental protection, health and education.

PRIVATIZATION

Nearly all small and medium state enterprises in Latvia have been privatized to date. Latvia's Law on Privatization of State and Municipal Property governs the privatization process in Latvia. A case-by-case approach is used by the Latvian Privatization Agency to determine how an enterprise is to be privatized. The three major methods used are: public offerings, auction for selected bidders, and international tenders. In some cases, a percentage of shares are sold publicly on the Riga Stock Exchange. Shares of certain companies which are deemed strategically important to Latvian interests may remain in government hands.

A set of performance requirements are in place for investors, both foreign and domestic, who acquire former state enterprises through the privatization process. Such requirements, which can be negotiable, are determined on a case-to-case basis and include the maintenance of certain employment levels and certain levels of investment into the company. The progress of each privatized company over the three years following privatization is reviewed by the Privatization Control Department at the Latvian Privatization Agency (LPA). The LPA decides whether or not a company is operating in accord with privatization guidelines, which are considered reasonably transparent and fair.

In recent years, the World Bank has assisted Latvian authorities in instituting a land title registration system so that it can efficiently restore land rights. In addition, in 1998 a Mortgage Law was issued to strengthen the recognition and enforcement of such rights. Both private and public enterprises have equal access to markets and business operations.

BANKING

The first two commercial banks in Latvia were established in 1988 under Soviet rule. Today there are approximately 25 commercial banks in the country, the three largest being Parex Bank, Hansabanka and Latvijas Unibanka. Foreign banks may open subsidiaries and branch offices in Latvia; licenses for such enterprises are issued in the same manner that they would be to domestic banks. Foreign banks represent approximately two-thirds of Latvia's bank capital. The local banking system is well developed, while most Latvian banks offer a variety of banking products and services, including internet banking and the international accounting system SWIFT which provides standardization, effectiveness, and security. The Financial and Capital Market Commission (FCMC) oversees the financial and capital market and the activities of its participants. The Latvian banking and insurance market is dominated by leading regional players such as Sweden's ForeningsSparbanken SEB, Germany's Nord/LB, and Finland's Nordea, all of whom are either owners of, or majority shareholders in, banking operations initially established locally.

The commercial banking regulatory framework incorporates all principal requirements of EU directives, while some banking regulations, such as capital adequacy and loan-loss provisions, even exceed EU requirements. In 2001, the Securities Market Commission, the Insurance Inspectorate, and the Bank of Latvia's Banking Supervision Department were replaced by a unified capital and financial markets regulator. Latvian banking legislation includes provisions on accounting and financial statements which require strict adherence to the international accounting standards. Such legislation includes minimal initial capital requirements, capital adequacy requirements, large exposures, restrictions on insider lending, open foreign exchange positions and loan-loss provisions. In 1998 an Anti-Money Laundering Law and Deposit Insurance Law was adopted. In addition, an independent anti-money laundering unit now operates in close cooperation with the Prosecutor General's Office.

Bank of Latvia regulations are based on international monitoring requirements set by the Basle Committee, EU Directives, and International Accounting Standards. The Bank of Latvia must issue permission for a foreign bank to open a representative office, bank branch, or merge with a local Latvian bank under the country's law on Credit Institutions. The five largest banks in terms of assets are Parex Bank, Unibanka, Hansabanka, Rietumu Bank, and Latvijas Krajbanka (Savings Bank). Other major commercial banks include the A/S Vereinsbank Riga, Hansa Leasing and Pirma Banka. Local bank loans are available to foreign investors, and the Latvian government does not interfere with the free flow of financial resources or the allocation of credit. A lingering perception that many of Latvia's banks facilitate illicit activity could damage the country's vibrant financial sector. Nonetheless, Latvia's central bank has managed to maintain strong credibility, and Latvia runs an arrangement similar to a currency board, under which the central bank's foreign-exchange reserves cover the monetary base completely.

As a result of the Russian financial crisis, Latvian banks in 1998 lost a considerable number of Russian customers, the banks' investments in Russian government short-term securities (GKO) failed, and reserves for loans issued to Latvian producers focusing on the Russian market had to be set aside. However, by the end of 1999 the banking system had fully recovered and financial experts maintain that the Russian financial collapse also had positive effects on the Latvian banking sector, as it forced increased competition on the domestic market which proved to be a powerful incentive for the banking sector to consolidate as well as seek experienced western business partners.

A similar crisis in the banking sector seems unlikely in the near future, mainly because of the high degree of foreign ownership. Turbulence in the exchange rate also seems fairly low. However, this depends on favorable external conditions. Were Scandinavian banks, for instance, to stop or significantly slow new lending, the lat's peg to the euro could come under severe pressure and Latvia would then to be forced to abandon the peg. The impact of such readjustment would be severe, as around 70 percent of borrowing is now in euros. Thus companies and households are extremely vulnerable to exchange-rate risks. One scenario that would have eliminated such risk is entry into the euro zone. However, high inflation has already forced a postponement of the target entry date by two years from 2008 to 2010. There is also a risk that the new target will also not be achieved if demand-driven pressures do not abate, leaving the economy dangerously exposed.

CURRENCY

Foreign investors can freely convert local currency into foreign exchange at market rates, and investors should also have no problem obtaining foreign exchange from Latvian commercial banks for the purpose of investment remittances. ATMs are widely available in Riga and other major towns. Both local banks and currency exchange points are available to obtain local currency. However, keep in mind that some banks and currency exchange counters may refuse to accept currency printed before 1990, or currency that is crumpled, torn, discolored or defaced by pen marks. If they are accepted, a processing fee may be charged in addition to regular transaction fees.

The Latvian government maintains no controls over the import, export, use or exchange of foreign currencies in Latvia. Since 2005 the exchange rate has been tied to the euro. The Bank of Latvia ensures the external stability, free capital movement and unlimited convertibility of the national currency.

TAXATION AND CUSTOMS

The Latvian government agreed in principal in 2006 to reduce the rate of personal income tax from 25 percent to 22 percent in 2007, 19 percent in 2008 and 15 percent in 2009. Although the new policy has broad support in the parliament, its implementation may have to be delayed until disinflation is firmly on track. Corporate income tax is only 15 percent and there are no other local business taxes. However, social contributions remain high.

Foreign investors in Latvia are exempt from Value Added Tax (VAT) on the foreign investment of fixed assets for manufacturing under Latvian tax law, though this is contingent upon the importer being a registered VAT-payer in Latvia. VAT is applied at a basic rate of 18 percent, while utilities and certain other services need only pay 5 percent VAT. Business real estate tax stands at

Table 3.3   Paying Taxes, 2006

Indicator*	Latvia	Region
Number of payments	8	50
Number of hours	320	423
Total tax rate	42.6	56

Source: The World Bank, 2006, <www.doingbusiness.org>.
*The above data shows the tax that a medium-size company must pay or withhold in a given year, as well as measures of the administrative burden in paying taxes. These measures include the number of payments an entrepreneur must make; the number of hours spent preparing, filing, and paying; and the percentage of their profits they must pay in taxes.

1.5 percent. Payers of VAT are entitled to deduct the amount of VAT paid from the tax which they charge their customers. In the case of sales which exceed 10,000 lats (excluding exempted sales) within a one-year period, the investor must register with the State Revenue Service for VAT payers within one month. All investors are exempt from VAT and customs duties on fixed assets, which are imported as long-term investments.

Latvia's Customs Law provides for customs duty exemptions, including for foreign investors, which are usually exempt from tariffs on the temporary import of goods, though temporary imports into Latvia may not exceed two years' time. The tax rebate on real estate and corporate income tax cannot be more than 50 percent of the amount of investment. In addition, foreign investors in Latvia are entitled to exemption from VAT and customs duties on fixed assets imported as long-term investments.

Additionally, Latvian customs authorities may enforce strict regulations concerning temporary importation into or export from Latvia of certain types of items such as weapons or firearms, religious materials, antiquities, medications and drugs, and business equipment. The tax regime does not discriminate against foreign firms.

Duties exist on both import and export of goods under Latvian and EU customs regulations; however, the transit of goods through Latvia is not subject to import and export duties or Value Added Tax. Import rates vary depending on the country of origin as well as the type of the goods imported. Basic rates of the WTO, ranging from 0 to 55 percent, have been adopted by Latvia as it is a member of the organization. In addition, goods which originate from countries with Most-Favored-Nation (MFN) status or with which Latvia has free-trade agreements have separate taxation rates, while a rate of around 20 percent is usually applied for goods from countries with which Latvia has no trade agreements. Goods such as machinery and equipment, metals and chemical products tend to be exempt from tariffs or subject to lower tariffs. Agricultural products, on the other hand, are at times subject to higher tariffs. Art objects and antiquities, as well as goods such as minerals and wood products, are also either exempt from export tariffs or subject to lower rates than other products.

Gold, jewelry, alcoholic beverages and tobacco (whose taxes are usually paid in stamps), cars, fuel, oil, soft drinks, and coffee are all subject to excise taxes. The tax for petrol, oil, and diesel fuel can range from $160 to $340 per 1000 liters, while oil gases are taxed at a rate of around $85 per 1000 kilograms. Certain smaller cars and trucks are also subject to special excise tax rates, while only cars that correspond to EU technical requirements and standards can be registered in Latvia. Taxes also exist on natural resources and packaging such as glass, polymers, plastic, metal, paper, cardboard, laminates with metal or poly-metal components, pulp and other natural fibers. The Latvian government may at times lower tax rates on projects aimed at the reduction of environmental pollution.

Imported goods into Latvia require the following documentation: VAT payer certificate, invoice, a bill of lading indicating the amount, weight and value of the goods, the original certificate of origin and licenses (when applicable). To export goods, certain necessary documentation exists, including: a declaration, transport documentation, a contract, a certificate of origin, and appropriate licensing. Transit of Latvian goods requires the completion of local export procedures. Latvian authorities are currently in the process of easing the above procedures by implementing online services to submit declarations and other documentation.

There are over 60 customs warehouses in Latvia with storage terms that are unlimited in length. Products stationed there can be further processed in order to improve their appearance and prepare them for distribution or re-sale.

FREE/SPECIAL ECONOMIC ZONES

Latvia has several Special Economic Zones (SEZs) that provide eased tax regimes, including the Ventspils Free Port, the Riga Free Port, the Liepaja SEZ, and the Rezekne SEZ. Somewhat different rules apply to each zone. In general, the two free ports provide for exemptions from indirect taxes, including exemptions from customs duties, VAT and excise tax. The SEZs also offer additional incentives, such as 80–100 percent reduction of corporate income taxes and real estate taxes. Firms must receive permits and sign agreements with the appropriate authorities in order to qualify for tax relief and other benefits. These include the Riga and the Ventspils port authority for the relevant free port; or the Liepaja SEZ administration or Rezekne SEZ administration.

Under the Law "On the Liepaja Special Economic Zone" companies operating in the Liepaja Special Economic Zone, Rezekne Special Economic Zone, Ventspils Free Port and Riga Free Port receive tax incentives including: 80 percent or 100 percent rebate on the applicable property tax; up to 100 percent depreciation rates, applying the double-declining method for all types of fixed assets in certain instances; ten-year carry forward losses; 80 percent rebate on the applicable corporate income tax on income derived in the zone; 80 percent rebate on the applicable withholding tax for dividends; management fee and payments for usage of intellectual property; VAT exemption for most services and goods supplied in the free zones; and a minimum social tax paid by expatriates who pay social tax in their home countries. Such tax incentives are available for 20 years to companies selling no more than 20 percent of their industrial output within Latvia.

Table 3.4   Employing Workers, 2006

Indicator*	Latvia	Region
Difficulty of hiring index	67	34.2
Rigidity of hours index	40	50.7
Difficulty of firing index	70	37.1
Rigidity of employment index	59	40.8
Non-wage labor cost (percent of salary)	24.1	26.7
Firing costs (weeks of wages)	17.3	26.2

Source: The World Bank, 2006, <Latvia www.doingbusiness.org>.
*On a scale of 1 to 100, with higher values representing more rigid regulations.

LABOR

Both skilled and unskilled laborers are available in Latvia, while a high percentage of the workforce has completed at least secondary or vocational education. Many workers have a good education level, especially in the technology sector, and some may speak Latvian, Russian, English, and German. In general, foreign managers tend to agree that Latvians are hard working and reliable, and that the workforce is well educated for the most part. Nonetheless, mid- and senior-level managers with western-style management skills can be hard to come by, in addition to knowledgeable lawyers and auditors. Service-oriented companies have also reported difficulties in finding experienced staff, though the level of competence in such areas has progressed steadily in recent years. Some training, therefore, is often necessary.

As a result of high levels of emigration following EU accession, some regions suffer both from significant unemployment as well as labor shortages. Unemployment in the country is predominantly structural; some 40 percent of workers have been unemployed for more than a year as of 2006. In addition, many older segments of the work-force have Soviet-era vocational training which fails to meet the demands of a modern market economy.

WAGES

Tight labor conditions, high inflation and an increase in productivity and minimum wages and salary led to a steep rise of 20.4 percent in average gross wages and salaries in 2005. Real wage growth in the third quarter of 2006 stood at more than 15 percent year on year, well in excess of productivity increases, which averaged around 8 percent in the first half of the year. The Latvian government has argued that rapid wage convergence with western Europe is needed to check emigration, which is extremely high. The Central Bank estimates that some 70,000 Latvians, or around 6 percent of the labor force, are currently working abroad, mostly in the UK and Ireland. Companies must keep wages above a legally specified minimum, while full-time employees in Latvia work 40 hours a week. Wage levels are moderate though growing, with wage growth accelerating sharply in 2006 as the labor market tightened. There are generally five work days per week, but employers are allowed to schedule six working days per week. Employees are usually entitled to four calendar weeks of annual paid vacations per year.

Union influence on the wage setting process is limited, and industrial disputes are rare. However, both hiring and firing workers remains difficult, along with hiring temporary workers. Collective bargaining is primarily confined to the enterprise level. A 2002 Labor Law deals with discrimination and provides more detailed provisions on rights and obligations of employees' representatives. In addition, the law establishes a new institution that can be set up in the workplace called the Work Dispute Settlement Commission. The Latvian government is committed to adhere to the ILO convention protecting worker rights. An employer is prohibited from entering into an employment contract with a foreign individual who does not have a valid work permit.

MAJOR TRADE PARTNERS AND PRODUCTS

Latvia's economy is dominated primarily by the service sector since it lacks significant natural resources, save for wood. The Latvian service sector contributes more than two-thirds of nation's total GDP. The largest service industries are wholesale and retail trade, storage and communications, and real estate management. The second largest sector of the Latvian economy is manufacturing, followed by construction, agriculture and forestry.

Latvia is a member of the WTO, and has free-trade agreements with many countries, including the Czech Republic, Slovakia, Poland, Slovenia, Lithuania, Estonia, and Ukraine (not extending to food commodities). Latvia also has Most-Favored-Nation trade agreements with various other nations, including the United States, Canada, China, India, Australia, the CIS countries, and Hungary. Additionally, it has bilateral investment agreements with Austria, Belarus, Belgium, Canada, the Czech Republic, Denmark, Egypt, Estonia, Finland, France, Germany, Greece, Hungary, Iceland, Israel, Italy, Korea, Lithuania, Luxembourg, Moldova, the Netherlands, Norway, Poland, Portugal, Singapore, the Slovak Republic, Spain, Sweden, Switzerland, Taiwan, Turkey, Ukraine, the United Kingdom, the United States, Uzbekistan and Vietnam.

Several EU members are Latvia's most important import suppliers. Germany, Russia, Finland, Lithuania and Sweden are Latvia's main import partners. In addition, over the past decade, Norway has become one of Latvia's top ten investors, with Norwegian brands such as Statoil, Rimi, Narvesen, and

Table 3.5   Economic Structure

GDP by sector	Agriculture: 4.4 % Industry: 24.8 % Services: 70.8 %
Key Imports	Machinery and equipment, chemicals, vehicles, fuels
Major Industries	Agricultural machinery, fertilizers, synthetic fibers, street and railroad cars, buses, vans
Major export destinations	UK 22.1 %, Germany 9.9 %, US 8.2 %, Sweden 7.3 %, France 6.6 %, Lithuania 6.4 %, Estonia 5.2 %, Denmark 4.2 %, Russia 4.1 % (2004)
Key Exports	Wood, wood products, machinery and equipment, metals, textiles, foodstuffs
Major import sources	Germany 16.1 %, Russia 14.4 %, Lithuania 7.6 %, Finland 6.5 %, Sweden 5.6 %, Estonia 5.1 %, Italy 4.2 %, Poland 4 % (2004)

Source: CIA World Factbook, June 2005 – Latvia.

Cubus being household names in Latvia. Furthermore, Norwegian firms have more than 100 joint ventures in Latvia.

The country's main import item has regularly been capital goods, while fuel is Latvia's second most important import item. Chemicals also account for an important part of Latvian imports. The country has maintained steady export growth, with major export destinations including Germany, the UK, Sweden, Lithuania and Estonia. Due to the rich forest areas, main export items are sawed timber and wood products. Other exports include textiles and steel.

FOREIGN DIRECT INVESTMENT

The Latvian economy has been slow to move up the value chain, and more than one-third of export earnings come from wood products and base metals. Growth of investment remains high, aided by inflows of EU funds. Investment, however, remains too tilted towards raising capacity rather than improving technology. External imbalances are growing, with rapidly increasing indebtedness as a result.

Latvia ran fairly high current-account deficits throughout the late 1990s, with an annual average of 6.8 percent of GDP in 1996–2000. Such deficits, however, were primarily financed by inflows of foreign direct investment, since Latvia sold off most of its state-owned assets.

The emphasis has turned more towards borrowing since 2001, and foreign direct investment covered 84 percent of the current-account deficit in 1996–2000. From 2001–2005 it stood at 30 percent. Foreign debt increased from 22 percent of the GDP in 1996, while its external debt soared to approximately 112 percent of GDP in 2006.

MARKETING GOODS AND SERVICES

LOCAL DISTRIBUTION NETWORKS

There are few laws regulating the relationship between a foreign company and its distributors in Latvia. Many foreign investors appoint a single distributor or agent to cover the entire country, as Latvia's size enables one importer to carry products from several industry sectors. However, one should find a locally registered legal entity in Latvia, if doing long-term business in the country is the goal.

For investors dealing in food and grocery import and wholesale operations, a market that by now is generally settled in Latvia, dealing with a private food wholesale company will be necessary.

Traditionally, grocery shopping has been done in small, specialized stores, such as a dairy stores, farmers' markets, and neighborhood bakeries. However, as wealth increases in the country, so does the presence of large supermarkets or grocery chains. However, few large department store chains are present, with many foreign chains located only in the capital of Riga.

BUSINESS ENTITY OPTIONS

Latvian business information companies can provide extra information about potential business partners, and it is extremely advisable to find out as much as possible about a partner before entering into a business agreement.

There are three forms of entities available to a company wishing to establish a subsidiary in Latvia: a limited liability company, a joint stock company, a representative branch office of a foreign company. Permissible holdings for such entities are up to 100 percent in certain sectors with 49 percent statutory limit on foreign stakes. Latvian authorities treat branches and representative offices as independent legal entities subject to requirements similar to those of companies. For a foreign investor inexperienced in the Latvian or Eastern European business environment, a joint venture with a local partner can be extremely helpful. A company that is already registered with the

Latvian Chamber of Commerce and Industry can sometimes also be helpful.

A limited liability company, the most common form in practice as a result of fewer organizational formalities required, is established upon registration with the Latvian Enterprise Register, and has the rights of a juridical person. It may be established with a minimum capital of around $3,500 by a physical person or another company, and have up to 50 shareholders. In the case of a company with more than 50 shareholders, companies that make public offerings of securities, or those that are formed by the privatization of state enterprises, must be established as joint stock companies. A joint stock company is also established upon registration with the Latvian Enterprise Register, and has the rights of a juridical person. Since the structure and legal requirements for registration of a joint stock company are more complicated than those of limited liability companies, they are generally less popular. The minimum statutory capital is 25,000 lats, while specific types of operations including banks, insurance companies, and currency exchanges, may require more capital or approval of the Bank of Latvia.

A representative branch office of a foreign company is not allowed to carry out commercial activities (business for profit) in Latvia. A non-profit organization or branch operations without an office in Latvia can be established for approximately $50. It may be established for an initial period of five years. A fee for a bit less than $1000 is required to open such an office, while extensions can be issued for smaller fees thereafter. Such offices should be registered with the Register of Enterprises. These offices do not have the status of a separate legal entity. In addition, franchising has also become an increasingly popular option for investors since EU accession. In comparison to joint ventures, franchising has had less success in Latvia thus far, and is regulated under the Law on Competition.

All business activity requires commercial register entry prior to business launch, payment of registration fees, publication of the businesses establishment in "Latvijas Vestnesis", Latvia's official gazette, and approval of the Ministry of Foreign Affairs for foreign branches and representative offices.

Table 3.6   Launching a Business, 2006

Indicator	Latvia	Region
Number of procedures	5	9.4
Number of days	16	32
Cost (percent of income per capita)	3.5	14.1
Minimum capital (percent of income per capita)	26.1	53.9

Source: The World Bank, 2006 – Latvia, <www.doingbusiness.org>

Table 3.7   Joint Venture Case Study – Latvia
Company: Rimi Baltic AB, Latvia
Shareholders: ICA Baltic AB of Sweden 50 percent, Kesko Food of Finland 50 percent
Date of establishment: 2005
Number of employees (in Latvia):   Approx. 3,800
Main business: Operating retail stores selling food and non-food items.
Company developments:
2004 – Combined turnover of Rimi and Kesko Food exceeds 190.6 million lats in Latvia ($365 million), representing an increase of 41.8 percent over the previous year. The same year Rimi Latvia operates 10 Rimi hypermarkets, 1 Citymarket hypermarket, 33 Rimi supermarkets, and 28 Supernetto discount stores. Rimi hypermarket carries up to 20,000 food items and up to 40,000 non-food items, of which 65 percent are made by local producers. Some 3,800 workers are employed in all.
January 2005 – Rimi Baltic JV begins operating in Estonia, Latvia and Lithuania, announcing that it aims to reach a 25 percent market share in three years and report a positive operating profit in 2007. The Board will be chaired alternately, for periods of one year, by Kesko Food and ICA representatives.
March 2005 – Rimi Baltic operates 164 stores across the Baltic region, including: Rimi Hypermarkets 68 supermarkets, and 75 hard discount stores, employing some 8,000 people.
October 2006 – Kesko announces plans to exit JV and grant control over Rimi Baltic and its 200 stores across the Baltic region.
Source: Company press releases, local press reports 2004–6.

PROMOTION AND ADVERTISING

Printed and electronic media are one of a number of ways to reach customers in Latvia. Most Latvian citizens read the leading newspaper *Diena*, on a regular basis, and most Russian speaking Latvians read *Chas* and *Telegraf*. Leading business publications include *Dienas Bizness* and *Biznes i Baltiya*, both published in Latvian, and the Russian *Komersant Baltic*. A popular Latvian tabloid is the *Vakara Zinas*.

LEGAL REVIEW

JUDICIARY

Although Latvia's legal and regulatory systems both suffer to some degree from inefficiencies, legal and regulatory risk remains low as a result of Latvia harmonizing its laws with those of the EU; the regulatory environment is fairly transparent. In general, judicial institutions enjoy independence from political influence, and foreign investors do not face discrimination in the national legal system. The costs of bringing cases to court are generally low, and the quality of the system is improving along with enforcement of decisions. Waiting times, however, still remain a problem. Authorities generally impose few price controls and respect private property and contracts.

A three-tier court system was introduced into Latvia by the 1993 Law on Judicial Power. Judicial power is exercised by district courts; regional courts; and the nation's Supreme Court, which consists of the Senate and Houses of Court. The law also provides for Civil, Criminal and Economic Houses of Court. District courts are the courts of first instance in all civil, criminal and administrative cases, while regional courts are vested with the authority of appellate review for district court verdicts. Regional courts, however, are courts of first instance for cases specified in the Civil Code. Latvia's Constitutional Court reviews the decrees and acts of the president, and government and local authorities, to assess their compatibility with the nation's constitution and law.

Judges in Latvia are appointed by the Minister of Justice and are subsequently confirmed by Parliament, while Supreme Court judges are appointed by the Supreme Court president. The Supreme Court and Constitutional Court are independent.

In an effort to bring Latvia's legislation in compliance with the European Union requirements, Latvian authorities have amended the country's laws and regulatory procedures, while several legislative changes were aimed at increasing the transparency of the Latvian business environment and the regulatory system. However, massive legislative changes carried out in a short period of time have led to a situation in which certain laws may be subject to conflicting interpretations, while changes are badly needed to improve professional standards, expedite adjudication of cases, and strengthen enforcement of court decisions.

In 1958, Latvia became a member of the New York Convention on the Recognition and Enforcement of Foreign Arbitral Awards. Latvia can therefore enforce judgments of foreign arbitral courts made in accordance with the convention, as well as judgments of foreign non-arbitral courts under civil procedure law. In most commercial agreements today, many parties prefer to refer their disputes to arbitration rather than to the Latvian courts. Several arbitration institutions operate in Latvia, including Riga International Arbitration, the Privatization Agency, and arbitration conducted by the Latvian Chamber of Commerce and Industry. Arbitration courts in Latvia comply fully with international standards since the country's Civil Procedure

Table 3.8   Enforcing Contracts, 2006

Indicator	Latvia	Region
Number of procedures	21	31.5
Number of days	240	408.8
Cost (percent of debt)	11.8	15

Source: The World Bank, 2006 – Latvia, < www.doingbusiness.org>.

Law came into effect in 1999. The law also governs the enforcement of rulings of foreign non-arbitral courts and foreign arbitrations. The 1996 Law on Securities, the 2000 Law on Consolidated Capital Markets Regulator, and several other laws and regulations regulate the Latvian Securities markets. Protection of investor interests are ensured by strict control over participants in the securities market.

Riga Stock Exchange (RSE) bulletins issued after each trading session and securities market information on the internet ensure transparency of the market, while protection of investor interests is ensured by strict control over participants in the securities market.

Bankruptcy procedure is governed by two laws. The first, the 1996 Law on Insolvency of Enterprises, under which secured claims are settled separately prior to the liquidation of the debtor's assets. The second law is the Law on Credit Institutions which regulates bankruptcy procedures for banks and other financial institutions. The law stipulates that monetary judgments of local courts must be made in Latvia's currency, while local arbitral court judgments can be made either in Latvian currency or that of the investor.

RIGHTS AND RESTRICTIONS FOR FOREIGN INVESTORS

Under Latvia's Foreign Investment Law, domestic and foreign investors are both required to abide by the laws of the Republic of Latvia equally. However, under amendments to the law, foreign investors are prohibited from controlling companies that are involved in strategically sensitive activities such as air transport, security services, along with restrictions on lotteries or gambling. In addition, representative offices or branches of foreign insurance companies are restricted under the law to reinsurance operations, while foreign insurance companies are eligible to establish a full owned insurance company in Latvia.

The county's Commercial Law regulates business activities, and serves as the legal framework for setting up, managing and closing a business. The law also provides increased protection for creditors, higher accountability for managers, prohibits companies from using cash reserves to purchase their own

Table 3.9   Protecting Investors

Indicator*	Latvia	Region
Disclosure index	5	4.7
Director liability index	4	3.8
Shareholder suits index	8	6
Investor protection index	5.7	6

Source: The World Bank, 2006 – Latvia, <www.doingbusiness.org>.
* The indicators above describe transparency of transactions (Extent of Disclosure Index), liability for self-dealing (Extent of Director Liability Index), shareholders' ability to sue officers and directors for misconduct (Ease of Shareholder Suits Index), and Strength of Investor Protection Index. The indexes vary between 0 and 10, with higher values indicating greater disclosure, greater liability of directors, greater powers of shareholders to challenge the transaction, and better investor protection.

shares, and requires off-shore companies to disclose their shareholders. There are no performance requirements for a foreign investor in Latvia to establish, maintain, or expand an investment locally.

Under Latvia's constitution, the right to private ownership is ensured; both domestic and foreign private entities can legally establish and own business enterprises and engage in all forms of commercial activity, provided they fall within Latvian law. The Foreign Investment Law in Latvia allows for unrestricted repatriation of profits associated with investments.

Land and property can be purchased by companies registered in the Enterprise Registry of Latvia as long as more than half of the company is owned by either a Latvian citizen, and/or a Latvian governmental entity, and/or those from other countries with which Latvia has ratified an international agreement on the promotion and protection of investments. While foreign investors are allowed to lease land for up to 99 years, they may also obtain land and property in accordance with rules of the particular region. This excludes certain areas along Latvia's border area, dune areas of the Baltic Sea and the Gulf of Riga, as well as protected areas of other public waters, land of state nature reserves, and land usable for agriculture and forestry. Under the law on expropriation of real property, a very limited number of instances exist in which expropriation of foreign investment is possible. In such a case, compensation must be paid in full within three months of the date of expropriation. If such compensation is deemed inadequate, the owner of the property may appeal the matter with a Latvian court. However, there have been no reported cases of arbitrary expropriation of private property by Latvian authorities.

LICENSING

Licenses are required for the import into Latvia of arms, fuel, tobacco, grains, sugar, and alcohol as well as for exports of ferrous and non-ferrous metal scrap, ethyl alcohol, and spirits. Several fields of businesses in Latvia require specific licenses prior to establishing business activities. Such licenses can be from a relevant or local institution. Fees for licenses can range anywhere from $10 to $34,000 for commercial cross-border or national television broadcasting. Various fees are applied depending on the type of product import, sale, transport or business establishment in question.

A host of government ministries and institutions is responsible for issuing licenses for various product transport, activities and businesses. These include the import, export, and transit of weaponry, ammunition and explosives, licenses for which are issued by the Latvian Ministry of Defense; banking, insurance, investment funds, brokerage activities which require licenses from Latvia's Financial and Capital Market Commission; and the sale, manufacturing and services related to precious metals and stones, lotteries and gambling, investment company activities, production, sale, and import of tobacco products, production, import, wholesale and retail sale of alcohol, production, import, wholesale and retail sale and storage of fuel, repayment of value added tax to foreign physical persons for goods obtained in Latvia which are taken out from Latvia, and production of technical spirits. The above is all under the license jurisdiction of Latvia's Ministry of Finance.

Licenses for all activities related to drugs and narcotics are issued by the Ministry of Health; licenses for security and security related activities such as detective work, the import, export, processing, sales and repairs of hunting, sports, self-defense weapons such as small-arms and airguns, ammunition, explosives and electroshock devices are administered by the Ministry of Interior; air, sea, bus and rail transport of passengers and freight as well as the machinery involved in such transport, special aviation activities, underwater works related to ports and ships are all regulated by Latvia's Ministry of Transport. In addition, the Transport Ministry issues licenses related to postal

Table 3.10   Dealing with Licenses, 2006

Indicator	Latvia	Region
Number of procedures	22	21.4
Number of days	152	242.5
Cost (percent of income per capita)	36.3	564.9

Source: The World Bank, 2006 – Latvia, <www.doingbusiness.org>.

services as well as for wireless communication services. Licenses for wood servicing works and related products as well as licenses for the import or export of grain are issued by Latvia's Ministry of Agriculture. Finally, licenses for construction related activities such as management, design, consulting and execution of construction projects are issued by the Latvian Ministry of Environmental Protection and Regional Development.

INTELLECTUAL PROPERTY

Latvia has begun a process of establishing a modern legal framework for the protection of intellectual property in an effort to conform to EU and WTO requirements. Latvian authorities in 1993 passed legislation to protect copyrights, trademarks and patents, after becoming a member in January of same year of the World Intellectual Property Organization (WIPO), of the Paris Convention in September of the same year and acceded to the Patent Co-operation Treaty. In 1994 it acceded to the Budapest Treaty on the International Recognition of the Deposit of Micro-organisms for the Purposes of Patent Procedure. In January of the following year it acceded to the Madrid Agreement on International Registration of Trade Marks, the Nice Agreement on International Classification of Goods and Services for the Purposes of Trade Mark Registration, and became a member of the Berne Convention. In 1997, Latvia became part of the Geneva Convention for the Protection of Producers of Phonograms against Unauthorized Duplication of their Phonograms. In 1999, it became a party to the Rome Convention for the Protection of the Rights of Performers, Producers of Phonograms and Broadcasting Organizations, as well as the Geneva Agreement on Trade Marks during the same year. The following year 2000, a new Law on Copyrights was adopted which strengthened the protection of neighboring rights and software copyrights. Since then, the Latvian government has amended all relevant laws and regulations in order to comply with the requirements of the WTO TRIPS agreement on Trade-Related Aspects of Intellectual Property Rights, to which Latvia acceded by joining the WTO.

Despite the notable progress which Latvia has made regarding intellectual property rights and that the criminal law stipulates penalties for copyright violations, it is highly advisable to consult with a Latvian attorney before establishing an intellectual property right in Latvia. Several practicing attorneys in Riga are immigrants who hold dual-nationality and have been educated outside of Latvia or in an English-speaking country.

A patent or registration of a trademark is granted by the Latvian patent office. Requests for such a grant can be made directly or through a legal representative in any one of the following languages: Latvian, English, Russian, or

German. Intellectual property rights can be enforced through Latvian court action, while patents or trademarks can be invalidated by the court if they do not meet legal requirements. Foreign owners may also seek redress for violation of their intellectual property rights through the appellation council at the Latvian Patent Office.

Interested parties can request that use of the pirated works be prohibited and that known existing ones be destroyed. In addition, they can request compensation for losses, including lost profits, from the courts.

BUSINESS ETHICS

Corruption and the perception of corruption in Latvia have remained persistent problems according to many foreign business representatives and non-governmental organizations, while the World Bank has rated Latvia as having a high level of state capture. Under Latvian law, accepting a bribe or facilitating an act of bribery is unlawful, and heavy penalties are imposed for doing so. Although administrative corruption is relatively low compared to other transition economies, bribe-taking is not uncommon, and ranges from low-level bureaucrats in a position to delay or speed up bureaucratic procedures, to high-level officials involved in awarding government contracts. In many such cases, government officials are rarely brought to justice for this crime.

Several laws and regulations, including the 1998 Law on Money Laundering, and a 2002 Law on Conflict of Interest were issued in order to improve the business ethics environment in Latvia. Some provisions of these laws deal with the common practice in Latvia of holding several positions simultaneously, at times in the public and private sector. The laws also include a list of state and municipal jobs that cannot be held simultaneously with other jobs.

The Crime and Corruption Prevention Council (CCPC) which is chaired by the Prime Minister and encompasses the Ministers of Defense, Interior, Justice, and Health and the Prosecutor General is the primary institution responsible for combating corruption. The Anti-Corruption Bureau, an independent anti-corruption agency, also exists to combat corruption, while the Prosecutor General's Office plays an important role.

INVESTMENT OPPORTUNITIES

TELECOMMUNICATIONS

Updating Latvia's formerly outdated telecommunications system was one of the county's main priorities after regaining independence. As a result, large investments have been made in both telecommunication and high-speed data transmission networks. Ever since 1994, when Lattelekom was established, the nation's telecommunication sector has been growing rapidly. Today, digital lines and mobile telecommunications services are considered some of the best growing sub-sectors.

Latvia has one of the highest mobile phone penetration rates in Central and Eastern Europe, with more than one-third of the population using mobile telephony (including pre-paid phones). In the late 1990s, the number of telephone subscribers doubled almost every year. Today mobile operators in Latvia are eager to keep in pace with the latest mobile technology and network infrastructure. Aggressive marketing strategies of new management of the companies significantly helped increase the number of subscribers as well as mobile phone sales. The number of mobile phones exceeded the number of fixed phones in May 2002. GSM operators also saw the potential of taking advantage of introducing m-payment and e-payment services so that customers can make monthly utility, TV, cable and insurance and other payments as well as banking. Many customers use these payment services.

One of the most popular cell phone brand in Latvia is Nokia, followed by Siemens, Alcatel, Samsung, Motorola, and Sony, to name a few. Latvia's two main mobile operators are LMT and Swedish Tele2. The former had a market share of more than 60 percent in 2001 with $48 million profit and turnover of $170 million. The country's telecommunications industry and internet usage are growing rapidly, boosted by the availability of cable services, ISP using fixed wireless broadband connections, and even mobile operators offering GPRS services.

COMPUTERS AND PERIPHERALS

Information technology is one of Latvia's most dynamic and rapidly developing industries, as the development of a western-style information society was deemed an important element of Latvia's strategy prior to joining the EU. Computer hardware is an extremely vital part of Latvia's IT market. The implementation of the Latvian Education Informatisation System (LIIS), in which every school in the country has specialized computer classes with access to the internet, gave a significant boost to the market. One of LIIS's goals was to provide one computer for every ten students in grades 10–12 and for every ten teachers, as well as one computer for every 25 students in grades 5–9. A National Library plan to link the county's public and school libraries by 2008 is also underway, with the help of a $500,000 grant from the Andrew W. Mellon Foundation. Estimates for the cost of the program's completion, however, stand at approximately $20 million.

New personal computers with the latest versions of processors, as well as small and medium multi-processor servers, are considered good potentials for investment return. In addition, multimedia equipment, LAN and IP accessories and related parts, as well as second-hand and overstock personal computers, are also rapidly growing in demand.

COMPUTER SERVICES

Software development has become an important part of the national economy. Most companies in Latvia are eager to develop their IT systems and take advantage of opportunities provided by e-business, requiring back office systems, LANs, as well as accounting and financial control systems.

The Latvian government adopted an e-Latvia concept and program, one of the most important elements of which is a system that unifies various information systems which have national importance, including the nation's population and enterprise register, the tax payers register, the road traffic safety directorate, and the information systems of various government ministries. Network security, therefore, has also become an important national priority for the e-Latvia program to succeed.

To realize these and other plans, Latvia has a need for education and training, internet/intranet systems and implementation networks, as well as support services.

DRUGS/PHARMACEUTICALS

As most medical services in Latvia remain in the hands of the state, a large portion of drugs and/or pharmaceuticals procurement passes through as state organized tenders. The retail and wholesale market of drugs and pharmaceuticals, on the other hand, is held by private businesses. As a result of the steady development of Latvia's economy, the state has been able to increase procurement of drugs.

Latvian authorities have prioritized the fight against HIV, Tuberculosis, and Tick Encephalitis, with many prescribed drugs that treat them, along with TB and diabetes. Such drugs are subsidized by the state.

An investor interested in this sector can open a representative office in Latvia or approach a Latvian wholesale company for cooperation. All drugs sold in Latvia must be certified by the State Drug Agency.

ENVIRONMENTAL GOODS AND SERVICES

In order to maintain EU standards, Latvia's Ministry of Environmental Protection has implemented several environmental projects including wastewater treatment and landfills. As the Soviet era left Latvia with a large number of heavily polluted areas, many services and products related to pollution control are in demand. These include: industry level ozone friendly technology, counseling services, wastewater treatment technology, pollution control equipment for oil and transportation industries, as well as radiation pollution control and nuclear safety equipment such as detectors and containers.

FORESTRY/WOODWORKING EQUIPMENT

With a long tradition and nearly half of Latvia's land area classified as forest, this sector is extremely significant for the nation's economy. More than 8 million cubic meters of timber are harvested every year from some 7 million acres of commercial forest land. Furthermore, nearly half of Latvia's overall exports are wood or wood products. Latvia's wood industry therefore has strong potential for expansion, as most saw mills are in need of upgrade or renovation. Technology, new machinery, and managerial and marketing knowledge are all needed in the industry, while raw materials and labor are available at relatively low cost in Latvia.

The Latvian paper industry also holds potential for expansion, with the Swedish "Sodra group" and Finnish "Metsae-Serla" accepted as partners for a paper-production project with an annual 600,000 tons pulp capacity.

Latvian pulpwood is exported to both Finland and Sweden. However, the need for the establishment of pulp and paper mills in Latvia remains strong, as the allowable cut of pulpwood exceeds mills' demand for both softwood and hardwood.

SPORTING GOODS AND TOYS

Sports have become increasingly popular in Latvia in recent years as disposable income and leisure time both grow. Substantial investments have been made in the sports industry to develop lucrative venues for recreational sports to take advantage of the changing circumstances in Latvia and offer Latvians the opportunity to enjoy themselves in hitherto unknown activities. Establishments that offer ice-skating, ice-hockey, golf, bowling, billiards have proved very successful with interest growing, especially in areas outside of Riga where such entertainment is scarce. In addition, the country's largely unspoiled environment represents significant potential for golf courses and other outdoor recreational facilities. Other sports and recreation related items such as pools and saunas are also increasing in their desirability amongst Latvians. Additionally, toys and games as well as children's recreational facilities such as amusement parks also represent investment potential for the nation's growing population, as there is currently a very limited selection for such products and services in Latvia.

GENERAL INFORMATION

LANGUAGE

Latvia's two main languages are Latvian and Russian, while most urban dwellers have a working knowledge of English. German is also widely used, though it is less popular. Translation services are available if needed.

COMMUNICATION SERVICES

Much of the time, telephone connections from Latvia to other countries are reliable, though use of international long-distance calling cards is limited and fixed-line costs remain high. It is necessary to inquire with one's long-distance carrier before departure whether such cards are available and known to work in Latvia. Prepaid cell phone cards, however, are available at the Riga International airport and in Riga.

Two major mobile phone companies operate in Latvia and generally offer good coverage across the country over GSM 900 and GSM 1800 bandwidth. Both companies offer internet connection through their network with a speed of up 43kbps. It is also possible to rent cellular phones from outlets or from the Riga International airport.

Despite the fact that internet use is increasing rapidly, Latvia has lagged behind the other new EU members in terms of internet provision and accessibility. Local internet cafés that offer computer access and fax machines are widely available in most large cities, while most hotels have e-mail terminals in the rooms and allow their guests to use the fax machine to receive and send messages.

MEDICAL SERVICES

Although Latvian medical care has improved significantly, it remains limited in several important respects. There are a few private clinics with medical supplies and services, especially in rural areas. Hospital services are not equal to western standards, therefore any major invasive procedures or surgeries in Latvia are not recommended. Not all antibiotics and prescription medications are available, while those that are will generally be European or Russian produced, though with different names and labels (usually not printed in

English). Diphtheria, hepatitis and tick-borne encephalitis are widespread, as well as multi-drug resistant tuberculosis. State ambulance service for emergencies is available by dialing 03 anywhere in Latvia. However, the response may be poor outside of major urban areas.

RESIDENCY

Foreign citizens can enter Latvia for temporary business activities for up to three months during one half-year period under Latvian law. If foreigners wish to stay for longer periods, they are required to obtain residence and work permits from local authorities. A passport valid for at least six months is required upon entry to Latvia, though no visa is required for travelers remaining up to 90 days in a half-calendar year.

For those remaining in Latvia for more than 90 days, including 180-day periods that cross over two half-calendar years, temporary residence permits need to be acquired. All travelers must also present evidence of a valid health insurance policy that guarantees any health-related expenses will be covered during one's visit to Latvia.

TRANSPORTATION

Road conditions in Latvia vary considerably from those in other parts of Europe, as Latvian roadways and highways are only now being upgraded after years of neglect. In many areas, even in major cities, inadequate road signs can be a frustrating obstacle for foreign drivers. In addition to poor road conditions, Latvia has one of the highest per capita rates of automobile accidents and fatalities in Europe. Oftentimes cars fail to yield to pedestrians, even at marked intersections, while driving under intoxication is a major problem. During the winter months, drivers should be alert for dangerous road conditions such as ice and fog. Spare capacity exists on Latvia's railway network, but bottlenecks and delays occur occasionally as a result of underdeveloped border-crossing infrastructure and bureaucracy.

If you are planning to rent or purchase a car while in Latvia it is advisable to inquire about specific information on driving permits, vehicle inspection, road tax and mandatory insurance. It may be advisable therefore to rent-a-car with a driver for people who are not familiar with the local road networks.

For those only staying for short visits or within a major city, several taxi companies exist which may relieve the inconvenience and danger of renting a car. Such taxis are not as reliable however in smaller towns. The largest international car rental companies are Avis, National, Hertz, Sixt, and Budget Rent-A-Car.

HELPFUL RESOURCES – LATVIA

Riga Stock Exchange: www.lv.omxgroup.com
Baltic Stock Exchange: http://market.ee.omxgroup.com/
Central Statistical Bureau: www.csb.lv/avidus.cfm
Latvian Investment and Development Agency: www.liaa.gov.lv/eng/
Latvian Ministry of Economy-Reports: www.em.gov.lv/em/2nd/?cat=6
Latvian Chamber of Commerce and Industry: www.latvijas-talrunis.lv
Latvian Privatization Agency: www.lpa.bkc.lv
Bank of Latvia: www.bank.lv, www.fktk.lv
Latvian Development Agency: www.lda.gov.lv
Customs Regulations: www.latvia-usa.org/latcustar.html
Latvian Development Agency: www.lda.gov.lv
Latvian Investment and Development Agency: www.liaa.gov.lv
Latvian Chamber of Commerce and Industry: info@chamber.lv
Latvian Privatization Agency: info@mail.lpa.bkc.lv
Central Statistical Bureau of Latvia: Tel: + 371 736 6850
Register of Enterprises: Tel: + 371 703 1703/703 1706/703 1791/703
    1792
Latvian Ministry of Justice: www.jm.gov.lv
Latvian Road Safety Administration: www.csdd.lv/en/Index.htm
Latvia Tourist Board: www.latviatourism.lv.
Patent and Trademark Laws in Latvia: www.alfa-patents.lv/home.html

Chapter 4

Investing in Lithuania

MARKETING GOODS AND SERVICES – 130

LEGAL REVIEW – 134

INVESTMENT OPPORTUNITIES – 139

GENERAL INFORMATION – 143

WITH THE HELP OF FOREIGN GOVERNMENT and business support, Lithuania has quickly transformed from an old command economy to a market economy since its independence in 1991, having embarked upon an impressive program of privatization. In recent years it has ranked among the top countries world-wide for business-friendly environments, while in a 2005 survey by the World

Bank evaluating the ease of doing business in 155 countries, Lithuania was ranked 15th. Despite the fact that room for improvement still exists, establishing a company in Lithuania involves relatively little time or cost. High marks were also given Lithuania for business regulation ease by the World Economic Forum's Business Competitiveness Index and the Heritage Foundation's Index of Economic Freedom.

Lithuania became part of the world's largest markets in 2004 when it entered the European Union. Located on the eastern shore of the Baltic Sea, the Republic of Lithuania, with 456 million potential consumers as a result of its strategic location and EU membership, has become an attractive destination for many new foreign investors. The country's proximity to the markets of the Community of Independent States (CIS), as well as Lithuania's impressive infrastructure, competitive living and operating costs, as well as its skilled workforce, offer foreign producers and suppliers an attractive opportunity to expand into global markets. In addition, a diversified economy, investment laws that conform to EU standards, a low corporate profit tax, a stable democratic government and banking system add to its lure. Lithuania has also been a member of the WTO since 2002 and joined NATO two years later. With the goal of joining these organizations prior to 2002, Lithuanian authorities speeded improvements to the nation's legal, banking, and tax systems. Additionally, economic regulations imposed by the government in order to meet EU requirements also spurred notable economic expansion.

Lithuania's private sector has been growing rapidly while proving its ability to adopt western business practices, compete in western markets, and demonstrate assertive entrepreneurship and initiative. Today, it has one of the fastest growing economies in Europe, and has demonstrated continued impressive economic growth and total factor productivity. The country has gained the nickname "Ballistic Baltic" and the "Baltic Tiger" from foreign business observers.

Furthermore, as Lithuania anticipates entrance into the Eurozone, the Lithuanian government has prioritized many investment-friendly policies, fiscal discipline, currency stability, and other measures to ensure economic growth. Anticipated funding from the EU of more than $12.4 billion over the next seven years to implement infrastructure projects will also undoubtedly prove extremely beneficial to the economy. Today it is one of the fastest growing economies in Central and Eastern Europe with international investors such as Siemens, Motorola, Philips, Philip Morris, Carlsberg and others, and a private sector in Lithuania accounting for more than 80 percent of its GDP.

POLITICAL BACKGROUND

POLITICAL STRUCTURE

The Lithuanian government is a multi-party parliamentary democracy with a 141-member unicameral parliament, or Seimas. Each parliament member is elected for a four-year term in a nationwide election for a party list, while 71 members are directly elected and 70 others elected by proportional representation. The executive branch of the Lithuanian government is headed by a president who nominates a prime minister and cabinet, or the Council of Ministers. Each minister is nominated by the prime minister and appointed by the president. The president, who serves a five-year term, also serves as the head of state and commander in chief.

KEY FIGURES

Currently, Valdas Adamkus serves as Lithuania's president, while Algirdas Mykolas Brazauskas serves as the nation's premier. Brazauskas' cabinet consists mainly of non-party technocrats and has emphasized the need for financial discipline. Other leading figures in Lithuania's government are Minister of Defense Gediminas Kirkilas, also of the Social Democratic Party; Minister of Foreign Affairs Antanas Valionis, of the New Union party; Minister of Interior Gintaras Furmanavicius, and Minister of Justice Gintautas Buzinskas, both of the Labor Party. In the nation's last election in 2004, the Labor party received 28.6 percent of the vote, while Working for Lithuania (Social Democrats and Social Liberals) received 20.7 percent and Homeland Union (Conservatives), 14.6 percent. Over the last decade, voters have shifted from opting for the Conservative party and the Labor (formerly communist) party. However, in 2000, a centrist party was formed when the Liberal Union and New Union parties won the majority of votes.

POLITICAL DEVELOPMENTS AND FOREIGN RELATIONS

In 1990 Lithuania became the first soviet republic to declare its independence from the Soviet Union, some fifty years after being officially annexed by it. Although by 1991 Lithuania became a member of the United Nations, it was not until 1993 that the last Russian troops withdrew from Lithuanian soil. In 2001 Lithuania also joined the ranks of the World Trade Organization, and officially became a member of the European Union and the North Atlantic Treaty Organization in 2004. Lithuania is also a member of the Organization for Security and Cooperation in Europe, the North Atlantic Coordinating

Council, and the Council of Europe. Today it maintains foreign diplomatic missions in 60 countries.

Relations between Lithuania and its neighbor Poland were tense following the suspension of two ethnically Polish district councils on charges of disloyalty during the August 1991 coup. However, the signing of a bilateral friendship treaty in 1994 and increased bilateral cooperation markedly have made ties with Poland some of the strongest today for Lithuania. A similar bilateral friendship agreement was signed with Belarus in 1995, while Lithuania later joined the United States and several European nations in urging Belarus to adopt democratic and economic reforms.

In 2003, the Lithuania–Russia land and maritime boundary treaty was ratified and a transit regime established through Lithuania linking Russia and its Kaliningrad coastal region. A 1998 maritime boundary treaty between Lithuania and Latvia has yet to be ratified by the latter's parliament as a result of concerns over oil. By 2004, a third of the Belarus–Lithuania boundary had been demarcated. Also in 2004, Ukraine's electoral problems were largely resolved with the intervention and brokering of President Adamkus. Notably, Lithuania's liberal "zero-option" citizenship law has substantially improved relations with its neighbors. Today Lithuania is free from political or security unrest, and has no belligerent countries on its borders with Latvia, Poland, Belarus, Russia and the Baltic Sea.

More recently, in what academics have called the "most serious political crisis" to hit the state since 1991, according to the *Financial Times*, the political scene was shaken by corruption allegations surrounding the family of Prime Minister Brazauskasm. The result of which was that the Labor Party leader, Victor Uspaskich, has been able to regain influence. Also, the balance of power has shifted in favor of Labor, so that if Brazauskas were to resign, there is no obvious replacement for him from the SDP. For the most part, the fate of the government increasingly depends on Labor's strategy. The government is likely to continue to enjoy a form of stability by default. Three significant accusations have been made against the Labor Party by *The Economist*: accepting money from Russia, kickbacks from EU grants, and breaching campaign finance limits in the 2004. The paper goes on to add, however, that such situations will improve as corruption has become a more important issue and public tolerance of it is decreasing.

ECONOMIC REVIEW

BACKGROUND AND PROJECTIONS

Since 1991, Lithuania's planned economy has moved rapidly towards its fully-functioning market economy today, in which the private sector creates more than 70 percent of all value added. Lithuania was ranked among the top twenty nations in terms of global business environment in the World Bank's report, "Doing Business in 2007." Low labor costs and rising productivity gave Lithuania a markedly competitive edge. Some 56,300 companies operated in Lithuania in 2004, with 95 percent of these being open or closed joint stock companies and sole proprietorships. The same percentage of all registered and active companies have fewer than 50 employees, making small firms the norm. In 2002 small and medium-size enterprises, most of whom were involved in trade, manufacturing, or services, contributed almost 60 percent of value added in Lithuania.

However, since the late 1990s there has been a noticeable decline in the number of small and medium-size businesses involved in trade as a result of rising labor costs and a stricter regulatory environment for smaller companies. In addition, rapid expansion of large grocery chains and shopping malls has also added to the decline phenomenon. Simultaneously, there has been an increase in the number of small and medium-size manufacturing and services companies, which currently offer good potential for small firm entrepreneurs in the near future. In addition, poverty still remains a major problem in the country, especially in rural areas where more than half of the nation's impoverished community lives.

The Lithuanian government has demonstrated its commitment to meeting the Maastricht criteria. As Lithuanian authorities prepare to join the Eurozone, inflation may be the main factor delaying the move. In November 2005, Lithuania's annual inflation on the harmonized index of consumer prices (HICP) used in the Maastricht assessment was 2.7 percent or 0.2 percent above the Maastricht ceiling for that month.

In a recent financial report, the Bank of Lithuania stated that "over the medium and longer term, the risk for the country's financial system stems from the existing imbalances in the real estate market, potential correction of asset prices, and a significant slowdown in the growth of the national economy." These issues are key aspects of macroeconomic projections in preparation of the budget for 2007.

Furthermore, the projections of economic indicators are based on the assumption that the Seimas will pass laws regulating general government expenditure and tax rates. An additional assumption is that authorities will legitimize the measures necessary for stabilization of inflation to be lower than

3 percent by the end of the year 2008. Fiscal discipline or adoption of the Law on Fiscal Responsibility by the parliament would help ensure such an assumption. Certain factors may reduce inflation in 2006–7, though realization of the risks emerged in the medium-term may slow economic growth. The prospects of economic sectors in recent years that faced a development boom will depend on their ability to demonstrate flexibility for correction of property prices.

The Lithuanian currency unit, the lita (LT), is expected to resume an appreciating trend against the US dollar, which will lessen import price rises in litas terms, especially for fuel, while prices of many industrial raw materials are expected to drop from 2006, further softening import price rises. In addition, global energy prices in 2007 are expected to decline somewhat from their current high levels, contributing to a slowdown of overall inflation in Lithuania to an average of just over 2 percent. Real GDP growth in the country is estimated at around 5.8 percent in 2006–7, mainly owing to a slight deceleration in domestic demand growth. Also in 2006–7, rising trade and income deficits are expected to boost the current-account deficit to an annual average of some 8.5 percent of GDP. Meanwhile, real lending rates are expected to remain low in 2006–7, with M2 money supply growth remaining strong, at an annual average of about 24 percent in 2006–7.

Economic policies are expected to remain broadly stable in 2006–7, while once Lithuania has joined EMU, full control of monetary policy will pass to the European Central Bank (ECB). The nation's 2005 budget continued to exceed many of its targets throughout the year, while during the first ten months of the year, the national budget (comprised of state and municipal budgets) fulfilled 86 percent of planned revenue, and 92 percent if EU funding was excluded. The only item significantly off target projection in 2005 was the inflow of EU funds, which reached only 58 percent of planned levels. However, as in other new EU member states, the disbursement of funds have initially proven slower than expected. This situation is expected to improve as Lithuania strengthens its administrative capacity to deploy such monies.

Anticipated growth in 2006–7 is not expected to close the inflationary gap between GDP and GDP potential. Such a gap, however, is expected to begin decreasing at an accelerated pace in 2008. GDP growth moderation is expected to maintain a sustainable average growth of 6 percent in the forthcoming years.

Lithuania's GDP growth strengthened in 2006, though it is likely to ease in 2007, according to the new EU8+2 Regular Economic Report. In 2006–9 and onwards a strong impact of domestic demand on economic growth will continue to sustain its positions, and positive trends of Lithuania's export indicators will be maintained. Nominal export growth will be stimulated by a recovered EU market. However, the need for modernization of production

Table 4.1   Forecast Summary, 2007 (percentage)

Real GDP growth	5.9
Industrial production growth	6.5
Average unemployment rate	4.5
Average consumer price inflation (year-end)	1.9
General government balance (percent of GDP)	2.0
Exports of goods fob (US$ bn)	13.5
Imports of goods fob (US$ bn)	16.4
Current-account balance (US$ bn)	2.6
Current-account balance (percent of GDP)	8.4
External debt (year-end; US$ bn)	13.8

Source: Economist Intelligence Unit Country Report January 2006 – Lithuania, <www.eiu.com>.

Table 4.2   Macroeconomic Forecasts (LT million)

Indicators	2007	2008	2009
Final consumption expenditure	72,935	79,814.7	86,530.2
Percentage share of nominal GDP	81.4	82.4	83.5
Percentage nominal growth	9.9	9	8.4
Household consumption expenditure	58,855	64,569.7	70,336.1
Percentage share of nominal GDP	65.7	66.7	67.9
Government consumption expenditure	13,841	15,054.5	15,998.4
Percentage share of nominal GDP	15.5	15.5	15.4
Gross capital formation	25,225	26,911.9	28,812.6
Percentage share of GDP	27.8	27.8	27.8
Percentage nominal growth	11.4	5.1	7.1
Balance of trade and services	-8,604	-9,899.6	-11,691.8
Percentage share of nominal GDP	-9.6	-10.2	-11.3

Source: Lithuanian Ministry of Finance, <http://www.finmin.lt/finmin>.

capacities of exported produce, and the increasing income of population, will promote import development; therefore, the commodity and service balance will remain negative within the projected period. In 2006 investments to machinery and equipment accelerated; as a result, the import of non-traded goods was enhanced and an increase in the current account deficit of Lithuania's balance of payments was observed.

BUSINESS ENVIRONMENT

ACCESSION TO THE EUROPEAN UNION

Since the accession of Lithuania to the EU in 2004, the country has been praised for its efforts in improving its legal and regulatory system. As a result, Lithuania's investment climate has been constantly improving as reflected in its economic boom. EU membership will result in more stringent environmental, quality and consumer protection standards which will translate into higher costs for businesses. However, such costs are not expected to deter further investment into the nation's economy, as the core of the local business community is expected to respond with appropriate investments to strengthen its position in the single market. More opportunities will now be available for those investors seeking lower risk investments and stronger rule of law. Indeed, since Lithuania's ascension to the EU, several large firms such as Morgan Stanley, Merrill Lynch, J. P. Morgan, HSBC, and CSFB have expressed interest in taking advantage of EU regulations to offer their services in Lithuania without opening separate branches there. Meanwhile, as competitive pressures on the EU from countries such as the United States, China and India grow, the regulatory environment in the EU is likely to become more business friendly as a result.

Furthermore, EU financial assistance will help create conditions for intensifying the investment process and in turn boost investors' confidence in the stability of the economy. Average final consumption expenditure is expected to grow by 10.3 percent in 2006–2009 as a result of accelerating growth of earnings, decreasing unemployment and taxation of employment income, opening EU labor markets and transfers of income earned to Lithuania. In addition, optimistic consumer expectations about economic development are expected to contribute to the nation's economic growth as well. Intensified consumption is expected to promote the growth of the whole-sale and retail market, though, under cooling of the economy by 2009, growth should approach that of other sectors. In addition, a marked share of additional income of the major part of the population will need to be allocated to increased expenditures on heating.

Lithuania's integration into the EU labor market is expected to deter-mine its development in a favorable direction. Currently, Lithuania's labor market is in the process of integrating into the EU single market. It is there-fore predicted that upon realization of any economic indicator projection risk, unemployment indicators will change only slightly. Emigration is not expected to hinder the rise of employed persons in Lithuania. The demand for expansion of the workforce, growing productivity, increase in minimum monthly wages and salaries and convergence of prices following EU accession, will likely have influence on earnings.

PRIVATIZATION

Lithuanian authorities have nearly completed the privatization of large, state-owned utilities. Currently, more than 80 percent of enterprises have been privatized. The local government in Lithuania has privatized nearly all major state assets; the eastern electricity distribution network and Lithuanian Railways are amongst the final major state assets that remain to be privatized.

Major infrastructure projects are currently underway or pending. These include upgrading the Mazeikiai oil refinery, decommissioning the Ignalina nuclear power plant, constructing the Via Baltica highway connecting the Baltic countries to the rest of Europe, and modernizing the Klaipeda sea port facilities as well as the Siauliai airport facilities. Currently, the Lithuanian government is considering constructing an electric power transmission line to western Europe, a natural gas storage facility, and a new nuclear reactor.

IMPORTS AND EXPORTS

In recent years, Lithuanian export destinations have largely changed direction from east to west, as the country's total of exports to the Commonwealth of Independent States (CIS) fell from 1998 to 2003 from 36 percent to 16 percent, with exports to the European Union increasing accordingly.

Although demand in the EU15 is still weak, Lithuanian products retain a cost advantage. The Russian market is also growing in importance, remaining Lithuania's leading single export partner; sales to Russia grew to LT 2.8bn, reflecting a 45 percent increase year on year.

Lithuania's second-largest export commodity – machinery – grew to LT 3.2bn, reflecting a 19 percent increase in 2005. Such growth was achieved despite stiff competition from China, as experienced in other European countries. Chinese manufacturing is also seen as undermining the textile industry in Lithuania, as China supplies both cheaper imports and is a cheaper outsourcing location.

LEADING SECTORS

The motor sector recorded growth of 17.6 percent, as car sales increased by 25.9 percent during the third quarter of 2005 as compared to the corresponding period of the previous year. Fuel sales, though, rose by only 7.1 percent despite the higher costs during the same period as motorists cut back on driving as a result. Non-motor sector sales rose by 11.8 percent over the same period. Large stores grew by 10.7 percent, while growth of small shops fell by 20.7 percent and medium ones by 3.1 percent. Meanwhile, growth in food, alcoholic beverages and tobacco grew by only 6.3 percent. Sales at large non-food store chains were up by 20.9 percent, compared with small shops, whose sales rose only 5.8 percent. Sales of clothing were up 33.5 percent, making it the fastest selling item, while household goods sales rose by 28.2 percent. So too, sales at restaurants, bars and other food service establishments were up by 23.4 percent, benefiting from increased disposable income as well as a tourist boom.

The slump in oil extraction has caused the mining sector to slow somewhat. Due to Lithuanian wages, purchases of textiles declined as the industry became less competitive for both local and foreign subcontractors.

The most important Lithuanian sector in terms of size was food production in 2005, which rose more than 8 percent on the back of stronger exports to the EU. As a result of strong fertilizer sales, the chemicals sector has also performed well. The strongest growth came in the vehicle sector, which in Lithuania focuses on trailers and bicycles.

Ekranas, a manufacturer of television tubes which holds one-quarter of the EU market for small-sized color tubes, reported a loss of LT 61 million ($22 million) in the first three quarters of 2005. In November, a complaint was lodged by Ekranas and a Czech company with the European Commission demanding that anti-dumping measures be adopted against manufacturers from China, Malaysia, South Korea , Thailand and Brazil.

Housing loan expansion has boosted construction, which had a growth rate of 12 percent in the third quarter of 2005. Trade and hotels had a growth rate of 11.6 percent, while catering had a growth rate of 11.1 percent during the same period. Both sectors benefited significantly from greater disposable income amongst Lithuanians, as well as increased tourism to the country. The third largest sector, transport and communications, posted a growth rate of 10.9 percent. Financial intermediation grew by 7.5 percent, while the insurance sector also showed impressive growth.

The growth rate for weighted annual average import demand in Lithuania's 20 leading export markets in 2006–7 is forecast at 8.4 percent, reflecting an increase of 7.7 percent from the previous year. The litas is also expected to strengthen as a result of euro appreciation against the US dollar and most other currencies in 2006–7. This, however, will have only a marginal dampening effect on the county's exports. Most Lithuanian trade is still conducted with the euro zone or with countries pegged to the euro. The litas will appreciate slightly against the Russian ruble, but Russia's demand for imports is expected to remain large along with oil prices. The strengthening of the euro is also expected to have a somewhat dampening effect on non-oil earnings by weakening their competitiveness, especially to countries outside the eurozone, notably Russia.

In general, Lithuania's exports and imports expanded rapidly in 2006. High oil prices pushed trade growth up, strong domestic demand also increased imports of consumer goods, while exports were boosted by Lithuania's success in fast-growing markets such as Russia.

Growing domestic consumer demand is expected to draw in rising imports of consumer goods, and strong investment will pull in capital goods. Import growth, however, is expected to weaken slightly compared with 2004–5 due to a slight rise in interest rates. Wages are expected to grow as unemployment falls, and labor shortages widen. Consumer demand during the third quarter of 2005 was the main driver of the economy in terms of expenditure, owing to an increase of real wages by 9.4 percent and of pensions by 17.6 percent. Private consumption rose by 12.5 percent (the fastest rate of growth since the first quarter of 2004) and accounted for 65 percent of Lithuania's total GDP during the third quarter of 2005.

Capital investment is expected to accelerate as Lithuania becomes more adept at allocating EU funding. Exports in 2005 grew by an impressive 12.4 percent as compared to the 4.6 percent in the previous year. Again, high oil prices accounted for the highest proportion of growth. Retail sales during the first ten months of 2005 (not including value-added tax) rose to LT18.4bn (US$6.4bn), reflecting a 13.9 percent rise in real terms.

The cost of borrowing in 2005 fell consistently in real terms and contributed to a boom in credit growth. However, the BoL (Bank of Lithuania) might raise the reserve requirements in an effort to stem this growth. However, room still exists for continued credit expansion with real lending rates anticipated to remain low in 2006–7, while M2 money supply growth is expected to remain strong at an annual average of around 24 percent. Lending growth is especially strong for housing. Subsidies from the EU have for the most part benefited exporters rather than primary producers.

In 2005, Lithuania's major trading partners were the UK, Denmark, France, Sweden, Poland, Germany, Russia, Latvia, Estonia, and the United States. Leading foreign investors during the same year were Sweden (14 percent of total), Denmark (13.5 percent), Germany (13.3 percent), and Russia (12.1 percent).

INVESTOR INCENTIVES

Lithuania provides special incentives to strategic investors. The criterion by which the national government or a municipality designates a strategic investor varies, though generally an investment of $50 million or more is required. However, other factors, such as jobs created by a certain investment, are also taken into consideration. In addition, investments in municipal infrastructure, manufacturing, and services may also be available. Special business conditions, including tax incentives, are provided to strategic investors.

BANKING

Under the supervision of the Bank of Lithuania, and the monitoring of the IMF and several international risk-rating agencies, the country has a strong and well-developed banking system which is considered well-regulated and stable, while conforming to the standards of the EU. The Bank of Lithuania also supervises all commercial banks and credit unions, while the Securities Commission supervises the securities market, and the Insurance Supervisory Commission supervises insurance companies. A universal banking model has been adopted in Lithuania to allow banks to participate in leasing, operating, insurance, and brokerage. There have been no bank failures in Lithuania over the past ten years.

The banking sector remained highly profitable, reporting a combined, unaudited net profit of LT 275.5m ($94.7 million) in the first three-quarters of 2005, a year-on-year rise of 27 percent. Growing loan portfolios accounted for a great portion of such profits, with net interest income reaching LT 554.5 million, reflecting a 25 percent increase. Housing loans, which constitute the main source of credits for individuals, stood at LT 5.5bn, an 84 percent increase.

The nation's commercial banking sector includes dozens of banks, including ten under license of the Bank of Lithuania, two foreign banks with local branches, three foreign bank representative offices, 61 credit unions, and the Central Credit Union of Lithuania. Large Lithuanian commercial banks provide banking services throughout the country through smaller bank branches, as well as maintaining correspondent accounts with commercial banks worldwide. Individual subsidiaries that provide mortgage and credit card services are also managed by these larger banks. In addition, company financing, investment services and foreign trade payments are also provided by these smaller subsidiaries. Lithuanian commercial banks also provide financing for exports with guarantees when possible.

The share of banking capital held by foreign investors increased to 87.5 percent following the completion of the bank privatization process in 2002. Today, almost all foreign banks are under German or Scandinavian control. In 2005, banks operating in Lithuania widened the range of e-banking services, strengthened their asset and loan portfolio, and extended payment card networks. During the twelve-month period ending September 30, 2005, the annual rate of growth of loans was 46.5 percent, year-on-year.

Access to finance in Lithuania is also much less of a problem than it has been in the past. Non-residents may freely open accounts with commercial banks. Bank loans, leasing, and increase in equity each account for just over 10 percent of investment finance, while equity finance is a slightly more important source than bank finance. Collateral required for bank loan averaged 114 percent of the loan value, while interest ranges from 3.3 percent to 13 percent. Loan duration is approximately 40 months on average.

CURRENCY

No restrictions exist on the transfer or conversion of the litas. The Lithuanian Law on Foreign currency allows for the use of the euro for domestic cash and non-cash payments and settlements. Lithuania offers unrestricted movement of capital and dividends. A Lithuanian currency board has been maintained since 1994. Prior to 2002, the litas was pegged to the US dollar at a rate of LT 4 to 1 USD, after which point the peg changed to of LT 3.4528 to 1 EUR. The litas is backed with gold and foreign currency reserves. In June 2004, Lithuania entered the EU's exchange rate mechanism (ERM II).

The Lithuania euro is currently set to be issued in 2009. The move is expected to benefit the country in several ways: risks associated with the present currency board would be done away with and financial ties with the euro area would be strengthened leading to greater potential participation in European production and stable sources of financing.

TAXATION AND CUSTOMS DUTIES

Lithuania is a member of the EU, therefore all import controls are regulated according to EU legislation. During negotiations regarding accession to the EU, most tax benefits to foreign investors in Lithuania were all but eliminated. Benefits for such investors, therefore, are limited to those applied in free economic zones.

Value Added Tax (VAT) is levied on goods and services at a standard rate of 18 percent, excluding certain goods and services under the Law on VAT. Certain goods or imports must pay an excise tax (which varies according to the product) under the Law on Excise Duties. These include lubricants, fuel, gasoline, spirit, beer, wine, liqueurs, tobacco products, coffee, chocolate and food preparations containing cocoa, sugar and products containing sugar, jewelry, gold and silverware, luxury automobiles, and publications of a violent or erotic nature. Tax rates vary. The taxable value of goods produced in Lithuania is their selling price excluding excise duty and VAT, while tax on imported goods is calculated by combining their customs value and customs duty.

Healthy consumption in Lithuania in 2005 led to exceptionally strong collection of VAT, intended to account for 38 percent of the total tax intake. In comparison to previous years, collection of profit tax in 2005 skyrocketed, though one reason for these impressive figures may be the fact that companies recorded profits ahead of schedule in order to reduce their payments to the "social" tax introduced by the government for the years 2006–7. Nearly all of the additional revenue is also expected to be spent on the social sphere, though as the recent higher declarations of profit tax in the 2005 budget show, many companies are likely to reduce their obligations. In addition, a tax on property used for commercial purposes is also being introduced, and real estate businesses throughout the country are divided over how this will affect property prices. The government expects that increased compliance with the lower personal tax rate will help to offset the total loss in revenue. Also, greater efforts to strengthen tax collection will likely be necessary to ensure that revenue growth keeps apace with the increasing burden of funding EU-related projects.

However, revisions to Lithuania's tax code do pose some risks to deficit targets; currently, the flat rate of personal income tax stands at 33 percent. This figure is expected to drop from 33 percent to 27 percent and then to 24 percent at the beginning of 2008, while local elections in late 2006 discouraged any tightening of expenditures. Other tax amendments, such as a temporary increase in the rate of corporate profit tax from 15 percent to 19 percent in 2006 and then down to 18 percent in 2007, also need to be taken into account. Additionally, tax on corporate profits will return to 15 percent in 2008. An annual tax was also implemented in 2006 whereby one percent of the market price on real estate used for commercial purposes is due.

FREE/SPECIAL ECONOMIC ZONES

Two Free Economic Zones (FEZs) exist in Lithuania. Both local and foreign firms operating in the FEZs have equal rights, including exemption for six years from corporate income tax and a 50 percent reduction during the subsequent decade, exemption from real estate tax, as well as a 50 percent discount on land leases.

One FEZ, located in the country's largest seaport of Klaipeda, has eight businesses either operating or about to begin operations with an estimated foreign investment of $410 million. The other FEZ – the air, road, and rail hub of Kaunas – was established in 1996 and announced its first investment in 2005. Accession of Lithuania to the EU does not allow for the establishment of new FEZs.

If a company's investments in a Lithuanian FEZ hits EUR 1 million, and at least three-quarters of such income consists of manufacturing, processing, warehouse activities, the company is granted exemption from profit tax for the first six years. In the subsequent ten years, it is granted a 50 percent reduction in such taxes. Meanwhile, companies are exempt from real estate tax, road tax, and VAT regardless of the amount of investment in the zone.

LABOR AND WAGES

Lithuania is a member of International Labor Organization (ILO) and adheres to its conventions. White-collar workers have a 40-hour workweek by law, while blue-collar workers have a 48-hour workweek with premium pay for overtime. There are minimum legal health and safety standards for the workplace, though employment regulations are often stricter than in other EU countries. Labor unions in the country are weak, and management – labor relations are relatively good. Few labor-related problems have been reported, with firms reporting no days lost to labor unrest. Lithuania has no tradition of resolving labor disputes through strikes or other types of unrest, and no labor strike has occurred since 2001.

Lithuania's tax burden (fiscal revenue as a share of GDP) is one of the lowest in the EU. Despite a favorable profit tax rate, such a tax burden is still considered, paradoxically, a major constraint. The country's social security and personal income taxes amounted to about 39 percent of gross labor compensation in 2003, and has remained fairly stable since 1996.

Lithuania's income levels still fall short of the rest of the EU, while per

Table 4.3 Lithuanian Labor Market Forecasts

Indicators	Unit	2007	2008	2009
Average monthly gross earnings	LT	1,671	1,868	1,990
Indices of the average monthly gross earnings		14.3	111.8	106.6
Annual fund for wages and salaries	LT mln.	22,209	24,893	26,615
Avg. annual no. of employed thousand people		1,529	1,533	1,538
Avg. annual number of economically active population	thousand people	1,608	1,612	1,607
Avg. annual number of unemployed	thousand people	79	79	79
Unemployment rate	percent	4.9	5	5

Source: Lithuanian Ministry of Interior: Lithuanian Ministry of Finance, <http://www.finmin.lt/finmin>.

capita GDP stands at some 48 percent of the average EU per capita GDP. In addition to this fact, the liberalization of the EU's labor market has led to a significant emigration of Lithuania's labor force.

The current monthly minimum wage, around $192, is set to rise to around $210. In 2004 and 2005, salaries rose on average some 10 percent each year.

Several sectors such as construction, health-care (nurses and specialists), transportation, and truck drivers have experienced significant shortages of labor. Although Lithuania's unemployment rate at the end of 2005 was the lowest since its transition to a market economy at 4.8 percent, employers still report a shortage of skilled workers and difficulty hiring foreign workers as a result of government restrictions.

FOREIGN DIRECT INVESTMENT

Total accumulated FDI was more than $9.5 billion in 2006 – a little under one-third of Lithuania's GDP. More than 74 percent of FDI stock in Lithuania comes from the EU, reaching slightly more than LT 13 billion, or $4.8 billion; 13.9 percent ($903.2 million) comes from Sweden; 13.7 percent ($893.6 million) from Denmark; 13.2 percent ($856.1 million) from Germany; 12.8 percent ($834.6 million) from Russia; 8.1 percent ($526.8 million) from Finland; 7.3 percent ($477.9 million) from Estonia; and 4 percent ($260.7 million) from the United States.

Table 4.4   Major Investor Nations

| | Foreign direct investment | | | |
| | January 2006 | | October 2006 | |
	Total (LT m)	percent	Total (LT m)	percent
Total	2,3895.8	100.0	2,4987.5	100.0
Russia	5,879.9	24.6	5,006.1	20.0
Denmark	3,791.6	15.9	4,063.4	16.3
Sweden	2,643.9	11.1	2,934.6	11.7
Germany	2,552.3	10.7	2,614.1	10.5
Finland	1,526.3	6.4	1,785.5	7.1
Estonia	1,776.6	7.4	1,747.7	7.0
Luxembourg	231.9	1.0	805.7	3.2
United States	654.5	2.7		2.8
Netherlands	704.9	2.9	656.6	2.6
Austria	517.9	2.2	616.7	2.5
Other countries	3,616.0	15.1	4,045.3	16.3

Source: Lithuanian Department of Statistics, <http://www.stat.gov.lt/en>.

More than a third of the FDI stock is invested in the manufacturing sector, while 14.6 percent is invested in financial intermediation, 14.5 percent in trade, and 12.9 percent in communication, transport, and storage.

INVESTMENTS ABROAD

Meanwhile, Lithuanian businesses abroad register investments of some $955 million. Investments into traded goods make up 46.9 percent of Lithuanian direct investments abroad, while 22.7 percent comes from manufacturing, 9.6 percent from financial intermediation, and another 9.6 percent from communication, transport, and storage.

Lithuanian investments to Latvia account for 43.5 percent of FDI abroad at $238.6 million, investments to Russia account for 14.3 percent with $78.3 million, investments to Ukraine account for 12.4 percent with $67.7 million, investments to Estonia account for 6.3 percent with $34.6 million, and investments to Bosnia and Herzegovina account for 3 percent with $16.3 million.

MARKETING GOODS AND SERVICES

JOINT VENTURES AND INCORPORATION

One of the best ways to start a business in Lithuania is to establish a joint venture with a local partner. Credit ratings and essential business data on Lithuanian companies can be accessed, though not always with ease.

Foreign investors have a choice between several types of business establishments: an investment agency, an agricultural company, a cooperative, a local government enterprise, a general or limited partnership or a sole trader, or a public or private joint stock company – the latter being the most common type of enterprise. Such a joint stock company can either be foreign-owned in part or in its entirety, while a new company can be established or bought into by a foreign investor. A joint-stock company is the only type of company that can be owned in its entirety by a foreigner.

A public joint stock company must have at least LT 150,000 (approx. $51,000) in capital reserves, while a private, or closed joint stock company must have a minimum of only LT 10,000 (approx. $3,400) in capital reserves. A public joint stock company must have a minimum of 50 shareholders, while its shares must circulate and trade publicly. A closed joint stock company, on the other hand, can have a maximum of 50 shareholders, and its shares may not circulate publicly or be traded.

An investor can establish a representative office to evaluate business opportunities, giving the foreign company a legal presence in the country without permission to conduct economic activity.

In order to conduct economic activity in Lithuania, however, a foreign investor must incorporate his business organization. To do so, an official address of the new company must be acquired, the name of the new company must be registered at a patent bureau, the memorandum/agreement on incorporation along with the by-laws of the new company need to be notarized, and minutes of the shareholders' meeting appointing the company's director supplied. In addition, a hard currency or litas account must be opened at a local bank under the name of the new company. The transfer of funds may then be allowed either from a foreign or domestic source into the savings account in order to meet the minimum capital requirements.

Before withdrawing funds, the investor must provide evidence of incorporation of the company. As part of the incorporation process, the bank issues a certificate documenting that the requisite funds (to meet the minimum capital requirements) are on deposit. The company must also be registered with a local municipality, and then with the Register of Enterprises of the Ministry of Economy. In addition, other permits may also be required.

In the case of a company which is incorporated outside of Lithuania, the registrant must submit several items, including: proof that the investor is legally incorporated, the most up-to-date audited balance sheet proving the investor's ability to meet the minimum capital requirement of the firm, a copy of the board of director's agreement to incorporate the company in Lithuania and invest the necessary funds, and a certified copy of the by-laws and articles of association of the investor.

Once the registrant submits a complete application and all requisite documents to the Ministry of Economy, the Registrar of Enterprises must issue a registration certificate within 30 days. All necessary translation must be made by an official translation bureau in Lithuania.

MARKETING STRATEGIES

As consumer preferences can vary greatly amongst different groups according to income, age and other considerations such as social affiliation, Lithuania's consumer products market is fragmented. In general, foreign products are well received by Lithuanians, many of whom in the more affluent levels of society consider price a good indication of quality. A distributorship arrangement is considered the best way to market foreign goods, and luckily, the distributorship network is well developed in Lithuania. One exclusive distributor should cover all of Lithuania, while suppliers generally set up sales offices supported

Table 4.5   Joint Venture Case Study – Lithuania

Company: UAB Philip Morris Lietuva
Shareholders: Klaipeda State Tobacco Factory and Philip Morris
Date of establishment: 1993
Local market hold: 57 percent share of the local market
Main business: Tobacco product manufacture

Company developments:
In 1993 PMI became a major shareholder in the Klaipeda State Tobacco Factory and established the headquarters of UAB Philip Morris Lietuva in Vilnius.

1994 – Plans revealed to build a $30 million cigarette factory in Lithuania to be completed within two years to produce the Marlboro, Bond Street, L&M brands as well as local brands for domestic sale and export to former Soviet republics.

1995 – Factory established in Klaipeda to produce Philip Morris brand cigarettes.

2000 – Operations in Klaipeda upgraded with a new tobacco processing facility.

Sources: Philip Morris International (PMI), local press reports.

by a dealer network. The relationship between a foreign company and its distributors in Lithuania is not regulated by the Lithuanian government, but rather by the mutually agreed upon contract between the two parties.

Franchise opportunities have thus far not been profitable enough to pursue such a technique, as local companies have shown little interest in them, with one or two exceptions. However, a growing number of affluent consumers who are brand-conscious may change this pattern.

Neither have Lithuanian consumers been known to respond well to direct marketing, as a result of a slew of fraudulent direct marketers in the past. Instead, most prefer to shop in stores.

TRANSPORTATION OF GOODS

Lithuania is thought to have some the best infrastructure in the region. Four international airports and excellent road and rail networks provide easy transport to the country's 3.4 million people. The EU plans will make Lithuania

Table 4.6 Business Procedural Ranking – Lithuania

Ease of...	2006 rank	2005 rank	Change in rank
Doing business	16	15	-1
Starting a business	48	44	-4
Dealing with licenses	23	22	-1
Employing workers	119	119	0
Registering property	3	2	-1
Getting credit	33	33	0
Protecting investors	60	58	-2
Paying taxes	40	42	+2
Trading across borders	32	31	-1
Enforcing contracts	4	5	+1
Closing a business	30	28	-2

Source: The World Bank, <www.doingbusiness.org/ExploreEconomies>, Lithuania.

even more accessible by the building of the Via Baltica highway through it, linking it further to the EU as well as to other Baltic countries.

ESTABLISHING A BUSINESS

Establishing an office is a relatively easy and quick process in Lithuania that should not take more than approximately one week. In addition, rental costs for office space are generally stable. Using a local real estate firm is the best way to acquaint oneself to available office space. A foreign company may open a representative office in Lithuania, which must be registered with the Register of Legal Persons.

Such offices, however, may not engage in independent commercial activity. A foreign corporation may also appoint a local agent. Lithuania's Law on Trade defines specific requirements for trade, while the national Civil Code covers all other agency related provisions.

PROMOTION AND ADVERTISING

International and national trade fairs in Lithuania are most often organized by the Litexpo Trade Fair Center of Vilnius, while the best way to advertise is to hire an advertising or public relations company. In addition, referring to Interinfo Lietuva's "Lithuanian Business Directory" is also recommended.

LEGAL REVIEW

JUDICIARY

The Lithuanian legal system stems from continental European legal traditions in accordance with the EU. The core of the Lithuanian court system (the Supreme Court, the Court of Appeals, district courts, and local courts) deals with civil and criminal matters. A system of administrative courts consisting of Highest Administrative Court and District Administrative Court was created in 1999 and generally handles disputes between government regulatory agencies and individuals or organizations.

Lithuania's legal system recognizes generally accepted principles of the legal regulation of investments, while foreign investors are subject to the same business conditions as are Lithuanians. Foreign investors also have the same rights as Lithuanians to participate in government-financed research and development (R&D) projects.

No major disputes between foreign investors and the Lithuanian government have occurred since Lithuanian independence in 1991. However, if need be, several possibilities exist for commercial dispute resolution within Lithuania's legal system: disputes can be settled in local courts or in the non-governmental Commercial Court of Arbitration, or, in foreign courts. Firms also have the right to appeal governmental rulings to the European Court of Justice under EU membership.

Lithuania is a member of the International Center for the Settlement of Investment Disputes, a party to the Convention on the Settlement of Investment Disputes between States and Nationals of Other States (Washington Convention), and a signatory to the 1958 New York Convention on the Recognition and Enforcement of Foreign Arbitral Awards. Lithuania's current Enterprise Bankruptcy Law was passed in 2001and provides a means to override provisions of other laws regulating enterprise activities, assuring creditors' rights and debt recovery. It applies to all enterprises registered in Lithuania.

Lithuania's government requires offset agreements (provision of services, creation of jobs, or purchase local goods) as a condition for awarding contracts for the procurement of military equipment valued at more than LT 5 million ($1.9 million). No requirements on local content or purchasing from local sources exist for investors, even for public purchases, though in some cases an investor may be asked to develop roadways or other infrastructure adjoining their project.

RIGHTS AND RESTRICTIONS FOR FOREIGN INVESTORS

Foreign investors are encouraged by local authorities to explore investment opportunities in Lithuania, while the Lithuanian Development Agency (LDA) is one of the main bodies working to attract foreign investment. Foreign companies are allowed to compete directly, or as subcontractors and partners in tender offerings backed by funding from the EU. Equal protection for foreign and domestic investors is assured under Lithuanian law, and no special permit is required to invest foreign capital in Lithuania.

The Lithuanian government has no right to interfere with foreign investors' property. In the event of justified expropriation, compensation will be provided. Lithuanian law also obligates state institutions to maintain commercial confidentiality. Foreign investors are free to enforce their rights by applying to the courts of Lithuania, as Lithuanian law protects the rights of foreign investments and investors. The local judicial system is generally effective at enforcing and upholding contracts. Investors may also turn to the International Center for Settlement of Investment Disputes under the Washington Convention of 1965.

When involved in privatization programs, foreign investors are also treated equally. Most state enterprises and property have already been privatized, in a process overseen by the State Property Fund. Foreign investors were responsible for purchasing most state assets offered for privatization since 1990 including assets in the banking, transportation, and energy sectors. Several complaints, however, surfaced by foreign firms regarding discrimination in some privatization deals as well as complaints of lack of transparency. The State Property Fund has been known to halt privatization when it determines that bidders are unsuitable after being screened for their performance. Several major assets remain that have yet to be privatized, including the Lithuanian electric power distribution company and the railway.

Representative offices and branches are allowed to be established in Lithuania by foreign entities, while no limits on foreign ownership or control exist. Capital can be contributed by foreign investors in the form of intellectual or industrial property, assets or money. Assuming that taxes have been paid, foreign investors are allowed to repatriate income, profits or dividends and to reinvest income.

Aside from several sectors, foreign investors have free access to all sectors of the Lithuanian economy. For instance, investment of foreign capital is prohibited in sectors related to Lithuanian defense and security under the Law on Investment. Any commercial activity that may pose a danger to the environment or human health requires special government permission, including weapons trade or manufacturing. Purchase of agricultural or forestry land is generally limited to Lithuanians alone, with the exception of organizations that have engaged in local agriculture for three years, or that have established representative or branch offices in Lithuania. This restriction, however, will be abolished completely by 2011 under EU accession agreements.

Foreign investors hold the same rights relating to commercial activities that local investors do under Lithuania's Law of Investments, including the right to transfer income owned as private property free of restrictions, so long as appropriate taxes have been paid on such income. Generally, foreign investors have free access to all sectors of the economy; however, Lithuanian law prohibits investment of capital of foreign origin in sectors relating to security and defense of the State. Both foreign and domestic private entities have the right to establish, acquire, and dispose of interests in business enterprises.

PROTECTIVE LAWS ON FOREIGN INVESTMENTS

Lithuanian law protects foreign investments in many ways, including the following: all forms of private property are protected against nationalization or requisition under the Constitution and the Law on Foreign Capital Investment; investor rights are protected under international agreements such as the 1958 New York Convention on the recognition and enforcement of foreign arbitral awards; bilateral agreements with several western countries also protect and encourage investments; relationships with financial and inspection authorities and the establishment of dispute settlement procedures are protected under the law on capital investment. The Civil Code of 2000 also provides several guarantee and security mechanisms to secure fulfillment of contractual obligations.

The *Official Journal* of the EU covers draft and adopted legislation in Lithuania, case law, questions from the European Parliament, as well as committee studies. A link to the standards reference numbers of pending legislation can be accessed through the EU's Harmonized Standards website, while the EU Commission's website publishes national technical regulations.

Government policies do not disrupt the flow of financial resources or allocation of credit, and no restrictions on credits related to commercial transactions or the provision of services, financial loans and credits are imposed. Lithuania liberalized all current payments and established non-discriminatory currency agreements under the requirements of Article VIII of the Articles of Agreement of the IMF, adopted in 1994. No restrictions on portfolio investment exist, and ownership rights to shares acquired by automatically matched trades are transferred three business days after the transaction is made.

INTELLECTUAL PROPERTY

On the whole, enforcement of intellectual property in Lithuania is weak, penalties imposed are low, and prosecution generally protracted. In 2002, Lithuania joined the World Intellectual Property Organization (WIPO). A year earlier, it joined the WTO. It is also a signatory to the other intellectual property rights conventions such as the 1990 Paris Convention for the Protection of Industrial Property, the Conventions on the Grant of European Patents, the WIPO Copyright Treaty of 1996, the WIPO Performances and Phonograms Treaty of 1996, the Trademark Law Treaty of 1994, the Berne Convention for the Protection of Literary and Artistic Works of 1886, The Rome Convention for the Protection of Performers, Producers of Phonograms and Broadcasting Organizations of 1961, the Nice Agreement Concerning International Classification of Goods and Services of 1957, the Madrid Protocol of 1989, and the Patent Cooperation Treaty of 1970 under the auspices of WIPO.

In 2002, Lithuania enacted legislation to guard confidential test data submitted for patent and trademark registration by pharmaceutical companies. After becoming a member of the EU, the protective legislation was also extended to designs, applications and trademarks of other member states. In June 2005, national law guarding inventions of a biological nature were brought into compliance with EU Directive 98/44. In addition, Lithuania is currently in the process of updating its Copyright Law to bring it in line with the EU directives on copyrights.

Registration of copyrighted works is not required, though to ensure protection of industrial property rights, registration with the State Patent Bureau (SPB) is. Trademark registration is valid for one decade from the date of application in Lithuania. No restrictions exist on the number of times a trademark may be renewed. Industrial design patents for foreigners must be secured by applying to the SPB with the help of a patent attorney registered in Lithuania. Protection for industrial design is valid for five years, while patents can be extended for a maximum of four successive five-year terms.

Patents may be acquired in one of three ways in Lithuania, either by registering with the SPB, with the Patent Cooperation Treaty Organization, or by extending European patent protection into Lithuania under the agreement between the European Patent Organization and the Government of Lithuania. A registered patent is valid for 20 years from the date of application.

Recognition of a copyright and its legal protection in Lithuania is not subject to any local registration requirement. Foreign firms desiring to register their patent or trademark should seek the assistance of a reputable attorney experienced in IPR issues.

Due Diligence

Several companies in Lithuania provide due diligence services. It is always best to know as much as possible about a potential partner. Lideika, Petrauskas, Valiunas and Partners' "Doing Business in Lithuania," and Interinfo Lietuva's "Lithuanian Business Directory" are good ways to find out more about Lithuanian firms.

Expropriation

Justified expropriation on the basis of public need is allowed by the Lithuanian government, though in such cases compensation with interest is provided within three months of the date of expropriation. No cases of expropriation of private property by the government have been reported since 1990.

Bureaucracy and Business Ethics

Lithuania has made significant progress in addressing issues common to countries of the former Soviet Union such as corruption, inefficient government bureaucracy, and lack of regulatory transparency. Although corruption continues to be addressed by authorities, it remains a problem, especially when awarding government contracts or granting licenses and permits. Money laundering, tax evasion, and other financial crimes are also prevalent. However, major foreign investors report that corruption is not a significant obstacle to doing business in Lithuania, and that officials are generally helpful and fair. Nonetheless, with many governmental institutions regulating commerce, opportunities for corruption continue to exist.

About one-third of Lithuanian firms cite corruption as a major impediment to doing business. Also, bureaucratic red tape can still be a major cause for frustration amongst investors. Business leaders complain that bureaucratic procedures often are difficult to understand, inconsistent and result in needlessly wasted time, while small businesses report the need to pay "grease money" to obtain permits promptly. Small firms have more problems with informal payments than large ones, and domestic firms have strikingly more problems than foreign ones. Local companies routinely pay bribes, while service providers may pay small bribes to officials and later regain the costs in fees they charge clients. Despite the ongoing practice, paying or accepting a bribe is a criminal act in Lithuania.

Although businesses generally operate in an ethical manner, institutions ensuring ethics in business remain weak. Ethical codes exist, but are usually not very strict and there are little efforts to enforce them. Recently, the

Lithuanian Foreign Investors' Forum began promoting the concept of corporate social responsibility. Unwritten business ethics such as honoring oral agreements, not involving the government in competition among enterprises, and settling disputes without litigation, also exist.

INVESTMENT OPPORTUNITIES

TELECOMMUNICATION

Telecommunications is one of Lithuania's most quickly expanding sectors. The once state-owned company, Lithuanian Telecom, or Lietuvos Telekomas, is now controlled by a group of shareholders. Today, only 2 percent of the company is held by the government, while Amber Teleholdings holds 60 percent. The remaining shareholders each control no more than 7 percent of the firm. Three additional companies – Bite-GSM, Omnitel, and Tele-2 – are also major players in the industry.

Telephone access stands at 236 landlines per 1,000 people, close to the regional average. In July 2005, average mobile communications in Lithuania was higher than both the EU and Baltic states, with an impressive 83 percent penetration rate. In December 2005, according to statistics of business intelligence provider Informa Telecoms & Media, Lithuania had the world's highest mobile penetration, reaching 138.53 percent and exceeding Luxembourg (131.95 percent), Barbados (131.1 percent) and the Netherlands (128.04 percent).

The Lithuanian government intends to further liberalize its telecommunications market by establishing conditions for improving communications and by lowering the number of licenses required. Electronic trade payments will be implemented, digital television and radio systems introduced, and national communications and information services expanded.

Furthermore, Lithuania's communications and information network will continue to be integrated into European and international communications systems. Meanwhile, demand for the internet is rapidly expanding in the Lithuanian public sector and educational institutions specifically, thus opening opportunities for investment in service and equipment supply.

INTERNET TECHNOLOGY

Despite its small size, the Lithuanian IT market is quickly expanding, with its development a top strategic goal of both the public and private sectors. An IT infrastructure development program already exists in the public sector, while a growing number of businesses have installed corporate LANs and WANs. Lithuania ranks 17 out of 25 in the EU in terms of Broadband penetration, with an average penetration rate of only about one-third of the EU. Broadband internet access is currently available to the nearly 2.3 million Lithuanian city dwellers, while subscribers to the internet tripled during 2004, reaching more than a half million in 2005. The Communications Regulatory Authority predicts further expansion of internet penetration at a growing pace in the future. Meeting the demands of an expanding information society has been the goal of the nation's IT sector, while demand for software development and consulting is growing fast.

Many private consumers have also begun purchasing computers and computer accessories, and personal computers sales increased significantly in 2005 as a result of tax incentives that provide personal income tax deductions for PC purchases from 2004–6.

A well developed computer and computer peripherals market exists in the country, including firms such as Microsoft, IBM, HP, and Compaq, which supply both hardware and software. Some 20 computer companies, out of a total of 400, currently dominate the market, with US equipment accounting for some 80 percent of total annual imports.

Powerful multi-media processors, networking equipment, and internet and e-commerce application software are considered promising for IT exports from Lithuania, especially since the demand for such products is growing quickly in countries surrounding Lithuania. Currently, a mere 0.3 percent of Lithuania's exports consist of IT goods and services, leaving a substantial amount of growth potential for the sector.

POWER AND RENEWABLE ENERGY

Lithuania is currently in the process of restructuring and privatizing its energy sector. In December 2004 Lithuania closed its first nuclear power plant, while a second, the Ignalina nuclear power plant, which provides up to 90 percent of the nation's power, is in the process of being decommissioned under an agreement with the EU. Lithuania is presently a net exporter of petro-chemicals and electricity, as the capacity of its power plants and oil refineries exceeds domestic demand. Despite this fact, electricity exports have fallen significantly since the closure of its first nuclear reactor.

Lithuania launched an energy transmission line project in 1998 to liber-alize its electricity market and integrate the Baltic States' power grid with the European market. However, the construction of a power bridge project with Poland was put on hold, in addition to an underwater power bridge project with Sweden. High-voltage (330kv) overhead lines interconnect Lithuania's energy systems, which operate in parallel with Russian, Belarusian, Latvian and Estonian power systems.

Nearly 60 percent of Lithuania's energy resources such as nuclear fuel, oil, gas and coal are imported. Natural gas is imported from Russia, as Lithuania has no gas fields. Gas accounts for 22 percent of Lithuania's energy demand, with thermal energy plants and the chemical industry being the largest consumers of natural gas. The construction of a gas storage facility to maintain reserves is currently being considered by Lithuanian authorities.

Several opportunities exist within the Lithuanian power-generation sector for foreign technology and service companies. The decommissioning of the Ignalina Nuclear Power Plant's reactors and the tentative construction of a new power plant, restructuring, privatization and modernization of state-owned power generation companies, construction of natural gas storage facilities and the modernization and expansion of the country's gas distribution network, development of renewable energy sources, and the construction of electric power lines in the western portion of the country, are just some of the projects which offer investment opportunities.

Environmental Goods and Services

Approximately $50 million will be needed annually by 2015 for Lithuania to comply with EU environmental requirements that the Lithuanian Ministry of the Environment must meet, making environmental protection a priority in the national Public Investment Program. Most of this sum will be spent on improving wastewater treatment and sewage and waste management, thereby creating potential opportunities for investment in waste disposal and environmental monitoring, remediation and protection.

Lithuania's industrial development increased the urgency of addressing the country's environmental problems, and led to the establishment of Lithuania's environmental protection program, launched in 1992. The program prioritized all major environmental problems in the country, and added policies to its legal framework on pollution cleanup and prevention in 1995.

Foreign environmental consulting companies seem to be more active than equipment manufacturers and suppliers in this sector. There are substantial opportunities for environmental service providers willing to team up with local partners. Such opportunities include laboratory chemical analysis, site assessment, soil and groundwater remediation, environmental impact consulting, and services related to hazardous and other waste management.

Construction and Regeneration

In 2005, the Lithuanian Association of Construction Companies estimated Lithuania's construction market at $2.1 billion, making it one of the fastest growing in the nation. With the introduction of private ownership in Lithuania, significant renovation and construction projects began, while upward trends in and growing availability of credit also added to the sector's growth.

Additionally, more than $12 billion that the EU will provide Lithuania over the next several years will further add to the growth of the sector by partially funding the renovation of roads, reconstruction of railways, seaports and airports, as well as constructing new nature preservation facilities.

Therefore, almost all products related to construction – such as tools, machinery, plumbing equipment, lighting, windows, heating systems, paints and doors – are in high demand.

AGRICULTURE

A net importer of food products, Lithuania imports goods such as fruits and vegetables, tea and coffee, beverages, meat products, fruits and feed grains. Exports to Lithuania in 2004 included wines and liquors, vegetables, nuts, dried fruits, and oilseeds. Foreign products such as wines and liquors, fresh and dried fruits, nuts and pet foods are currently available in Lithuanian retail stores and have good market potential. However, tariffs on non-EU agricultural imports hinder the potential for many products to succeed in the Lithuanian market. Exports from Lithuania abroad, on the other hand, included fish, meat, beverages and milk.

Some $3 billion in funding from the EU under the EU's Common Agricultural Policy (CAP) over the next several years will also undoubtedly boost Lithuania's agricultural sector. From 2004 to 2006, the EU spent some $80 million on agricultural investment projects including machinery and equipment purchases, and building renovation and construction.

Millions of dollars will also be supplied to farmers under Lithuania's Rural Development Plan for projects such as reforestation of agricultural land and restructuring of farms.

PUBLIC PROCUREMENT

Monitoring and coordination of all public procurement in Lithuanian is handled by the office of Public Procurement Office, which reports directly to the government.

Potentially worthwhile opportunities for foreign suppliers and service providers are in the energy, defense, communication and transportation sectors, as well as in environmental protection.

Most announcements for public tender are published in Lithuanian in the government's official newspaper, *Valstybes Zinios*, under the information supplement.

GENERAL INFORMATION

LANGUAGE

The people of Lithuania speak one of the oldest surviving Baltic languages, though most Lithuanians also speak Russian, and many younger ones speak English.

LOCAL CUSTOMS

Social and business customs are quite similar in Lithuania to much of northern Europe. Credit cards (Mastercard and Visa mostly) are accepted at most hotels and quality restaurants. In rural areas though, travelers are advised to be equipped with enough cash in case credit cards are not accepted.

COMMUNICATION SERVICES

Communications systems in Lithuania are generally superb, with domestic and international phone, mobile phones, faxes, and e-mail accessibility. Limited connectivity is sometimes reported in rural areas depending on service providers. Internet sites for Telekomas, Omnitel, Bite, tele2, and the Lithuanian Development Agency can provide more in depth information about specific areas and communication in Lithuania.

RESIDENCY

Foreigners are not allowed to stay in Lithuania for more than three months without a visa, and no more than 180 days per calendar year. Some foreign residents have experienced difficulty in obtaining and renewing residency permits. Overstaying a permit can result in fines or even deportation.

Obtaining a residency permit can be a frustrating ordeal, and while Lithuanian embassies are responsible for initiating the process of obtaining such permits, most often it is left to the traveler upon arrival in Lithuania. It can take up to six month for the Migration Office to issue a residency permit. Some people have been asked to leave the country since their permits were not renewed on time, while requests for documentation are not always standard or consistent.

Lithuanian customs authorities may require an employment contract for travelers entering the country for jobs. It is advisable to contact the Lithuanian Customs' office for travelers before embarking on a trip to Lithuania.

TRANSPORTATION

Direct flights to Lithuania are available from many western Europe cities. An automobile is considered one of the most convenient ways of getting around the country. Lithuania's Department of Tourism is a good source for further information.

HELPFUL RESOURCES – LITHUANIA

Lithuanian Development Agency: www.lda.lt
Lithuanian Ministry of Economy: www.ukmin.lt
Lithuanian Development Agency: www.lda.lt
Lithuanian Ministry of Environment: www.am.lt
Lithuanian Development Agency: www.lda.lt
Lithuanian Builders Association: www.statybininkai.lt
Ministry of Environment: www.am.lt
Ministry of Agriculture: www.zum.lt
Ministry of Finance: www.finmin.lt
Ministry of Economy: www.ukmin.lt
Ministry of Interior: www.vrm.lt
Ministry of Transportation and Communication: www.transp.lt
Ministry of Defense: www.kam.lt
Ministry of Justice: www.tm.lt
Ministry of Education: www.smm.lt
Ministry of Culture: www.lrkm.lt
Ministry of Foreign Affairs: www.urm.lt
Ministry of Social Affairs: www.socmin.lt
Ministry of Health: www.sam.lt
Lithuanian Customs: www.cust.lt/en/rubric?rubricID=188
Lithuanian Ministry of Economy: www.ukmin.lt
Association of Chambers of Commerce and Industry: www.chambers.lt
The Bank of Lithuania: www.lbank.lt
State Tax Inspection (Ministry of Finance): www.vmi.lt
Country Limitation Schedule:
      www.exim.gov/tools/country/country_limits.html
Trade and Development Agency: www.tda.gov
Lithuanian Development Agency: www.lda.lt

SBA's Office of International Trade: www.sba.gov/oit
Commercial Court of the Republic of Lithuania
Gedimino pr. 39/1, LT-2640 Vilnius, Lithuania;
Telephone: 370-5 2622843
Fax: 370-5 2619927

MISCELLANEOUS

International Monetary Fund: www.imflithuania@imf.org
World Bank: www.worldbank.lt
Litexpo Center: www.litexpo.lt
Infobalt: www.infobalt.lt
Lideika, Petraukas, Valiunas and Partners' "Doing Business in
    Lithuania": www.lawin.lt/book
Lithuania in Your Pocket: www.inyourpocket.com/lithuania/en
OPIC: www.opic.gov

Chapter 5

Investing in Kazakhstan

❖   Promotion and Advertising – 160
❖   Pricing – 161

LEGAL REVIEW – 162

❖   Judiciary – 162
❖   Intellectual Property – 163
❖   Licensing – 164
❖   Standardization – 165
❖   Business Ethics – 166

INVESTMENT OPPORTUNITIES – 166

❖   Mining Industry – 166
❖   Environmental Goods and Services – 166
❖   Oil and Gas Industries – 167
❖   Power Generation – 168
❖   Medical Equipment – 169
❖   Agriculture – 170
❖   Food Processing and Packaging Machinery – 170
❖   Building Industry – 171
❖   Telecommunications – 172

GENERAL INFORMATION – 173

❖   Communication Services – 174
❖   Local Customs – 174
❖   Visas and Residency – 174

THE GOVERNMENT OF KAZAKHSTAN has committed itself to diversifying its economy and creating a vibrant small and medium-sized business sector despite some difficulty in implementing reform. The country has made significant progress in recent years in transforming Kazakhstan's economy into an increasingly transparent, market-driven environment.

Economic liberalization and a major privatization program helped to greatly increase foreign investment. In addition, Kazakhstan is the first country in the former Soviet Union to have repaid its IMF debt in advance. Today Kazakhstan's banking sector is one of the strongest in the CIS and also a key strongpoint in the national economy. The country's significant efforts to create a sound financial system and a stable macroeconomic framework have been notable among former Soviet republics, while much progress has been made in creating and implementing an adequate legal framework. Inflation and unemployment have steadied though the regulatory environment remains restrictive. As Kazakhstan's economy continues its expansion, foreign investors will find growing markets for their goods and services across many sectors and realize the strategic importance of the country and potential for investment. In particular, investments in Kazakhstan's metals production, food sector and machine building industry have been rapidly expanding and have in turn led to a significant consumer boom.

One of the most important industries to the nation's economy has been its energy sector. Mining and resource extraction is one of Kazakhstan's fastest-growing sub-sectors, dominated by oil and gas. Sound financial management and foreign investments in Kazakhstan's natural resources have played an important role in the country's economic success and sustained economic growth for the past several years. Steps taken to develop a favorable investment regime in the nation's energy sector and utilize its massive untapped energy reserves (daily oil production output is expected to reach some 3–3.5 million barrels per day by 2015) after Kazakhstan gained independence in 1991, coupled with record oil prices, resulted in record export prices for its energy, minerals and agricultural exports. Additionally, substantial foreign investment in hydrocarbons is being felt in rising oil and gas production and exports. Furthermore, as the nation's energy sector continues to develop at impressive rates, foreign investors will also find a growing market for exporting petroleum drilling and oilfield equipment, railway transportation technology, and agricultural machinery and equipment.

POLITICAL BACKGROUND

POLITICAL STRUCTURE

The national legislature of the Republic of Kazakhstan bicameral government is comprised of the Majilis, a 77-seat lower house, and the Senate, a 39-seat upper house. Kazakh citizens over the age of 18 have universal suffrage for both the Majilis and presidential elections. Senators, on the other hand, are elected in part by the president and in part by the regions. The Council of Ministers is headed by a prime minister, who is appointed by the president.

No clear mechanism for the transfer of power exists, but there is no sign of political instability. Despite separation of powers in principle in Kazakhstan's government, the president wields nearly total control over all three branches of government. Kazakhstan's constitution has been changed several times since its independence in 1991, a fact that has led to the ruling by one man since then, Nursultan Nazarbayev. Although the constitution guarantees full human rights, freedom of conscience and social justice in principal, civil rights remain fragile in practice. Nazarbayev personally appointed a Constitutional Council to replace the more independent Constitutional Court.

In recent times, however, even the nation's elites have become increasingly dissatisfied with the limited political influence that they have under the current system. As a result, a growing number in government have called for greater democratization and accountability.

KEY FIGURES

Kazakh's current president is Nursultan Nazarbayev, first elected in December 1991 and then re-elected in January 1999 and December 2005. Nazarbayev's current term is set to expire in 2012. Until then, more political tightening to either allow him to remain in office or install a member of his family as his successor is expected. Kazakhstan's opposition is peaceful and democratic, though it is nonetheless subject to strict scrutiny and at times harassment by the regime.

Kazakhstan's former Prime Minister Daniyal Akhmetov resigned in January 2007 and was replaced by the former Deputy Prime Minister, Karim Masimov. The move was unexpected and had been anticipated for some time. The change in prime minister is not expected to bring about a more liberal political landscape or less interventionist economic policies. Kazakhstan's Minister of Defense is Mukhtar Altynbayev.

POLITICAL DEVELOPMENTS AND FOREIGN RELATIONS

The area which comprises Kazakhstan was conquered by Russia in the 18th century and in 1936 became a Soviet Republic. The area is inhabited mainly by native Kazakhs. Rarely united as a national unit, Kazakhs are a mix of Turkic and Mongol nomadic tribes who migrated into the region in the 13th century.

Under the Soviet "Virgin Lands" agricultural program of the 1950s and 1960s, many Soviet citizens relocated to Kazakhstan's northern pasture region to cultivate the area. The movement resulted in non-Kazakhs outnumbering natives in the area. Many of these newcomers emigrated once more following 1991, when Kazakhstan became the last of the former Soviet republics to declare its independence. A new constitution was approved in 1995 in a nationwide referendum which significantly increased the powers of the presidency and marginalized the legislature.

Today there is no armed conflict in Kazakhstan, however some risk of isolated skirmishes still remains on the border with Uzbekistan. Inter-ethnic conflict has largely been contained though some tensions exist in the north of the country between Russians and the ethnic Kazakh majority.

ECONOMIC REVIEW

BACKGROUND AND PREDICTIONS

Kazakhstan's policy process is generally focused on maintaining fiscal prudence and managing the exchange rate in the face of large hard-currency inflows. In addition, achieving economic diversification is also strongly pursued, though the task has proven to be exceptionally difficult. Free functioning of market mechanisms have often been obstructed as a result of interventionist policies for the promotion of certain favored enterprises. As a result, sections of the nation's business community have been alienated by Nazarbayev, who has remained popular among the Kazakhstan electorate.

Table 5.1   Key Indicators, 2006–8

Category	2006	2007*	2008*
Real GDP growth (percent)	10.6	9.7	10.4
Consumer price inflation (average percent)	8.6	8.1	8.0
Budget balance (percent of GDP)	0.6	0.4	0.5
Current account balance (percent of GDP)	0.5	0.5	0.5
Short-term T-bill rate (year-end percent)	3.1	3.2	3.2
Avg. exchange rate – Tenge: USD	126.09	127.14**	123.63

Source: Economist Intelligence Unit, Country Briefing 2006, <www.economist.com/countries/Kazakhstan/>.
*Forecast.
**As of March 2007, the Tenge–USD exchange rate was 124 KZT=1 USD.

Table 5.2   Kazakhstan Risk Ratings, 2006

Category	Previous score*	Current Score
Security risk	21	21
Political stability risk	55	55
Legal and regulatory risk	90	85
Tax policy risk	81	81
Labor market risk	50	50
Infrastructure risk	81	81
Overall risk assessment	64	60

Source: Economist Intelligence Unit, Risk Briefing , Kazakhstan – 2006.
*(100 = most risky).

Nonetheless, real GDP growth in 2006 was much stronger than expected, reaching 10.4 percent year on year in January – September despite a shaky start. Preliminary official estimates put 2006 real GDP growth at 10.6 percent. Expectations for 2007 real GDP growth are down marginally from 9.9 percent to 9.7 percent.

Industry observers predict that high oil prices, as well as large investment inflows and export volumes to offset any drop in the cost of oil will enable the government to maintain public expenditure at over 20 percent of GDP, while the Kazakh economy will grow at an average annual rate of over 10 percent in real terms from 2007 to 2011. Private consumption growth is also expected to be maintained, which will in turn boost retail sales and construction. Average annual deficits of around 5 percent of GDP on both the income and services accounts are also predicted.

It is expected that the National Bank of Kazakhstan will seek to reduce inflation by means of a more flexible exchange-rate policy for the local currency, the Tenge (KZT), and tighter credit policies. Large-scale capital inflows, however, will preclude significant disinflation over the medium term. Corporate law remains poorly developed and enforced though some progress has been made in recent years.

BUSINESS ENVIRONMENT

OVERVIEW

Foreign investments were severely lacking when Kazakhstan gained independence in the 1990s. As a result, the first Law on Investments was issued in order to draw foreign capital to the country. Under the law, foreign investors were granted a relatively high level of protection, including protection for ten years from changes in Kazakh legislation that would adversely affect a foreign investor. As a result, a significant number of investors entered the market by 2000. In 2003 a new Law on Investment replaced older ones and offered equal legal regimes for domestic and foreign investors.

Today, many foreign firms are active throughout the country, while a growing number of service sector firms including the Big Four accounting firms, Citibank and American Express Bank are present. Additional prestigious organizations, such as Ernst & Young, which in 1992 became the first professional services organization to establish its presence in Central Asia when it opened an office in Kazakhstan, are also expanding their presence in the country. Others companies, in telecom and consumer goods, to name a few, are also gaining a footing.

Also adding to its economic strength are Kazakhstan's significant oil and natural gas reserves, with proven reserves estimated between 9 billion and 17.6 billion barrels (1.2 billion tons and 2.4 billion tons) of oil and proven natural gas reserves of 65 trillion cubic feet to 70 trillion cubic feet (1.84 trillion cubic meters to 1.98 trillion cubic meters). However, environmental degradation around former Soviet nuclear test facilities and environmental problems surrounding the Aral Sea continue to drain national resources.

Despite Kazakhstan's prospects, however, many concerns continue to exist for foreign investors, especially those concerning attempts by the Kazakhstan government to re-interpret existing contracts, particularly in the oil, gas and electricity generation sectors. Furthermore, unevenly enforced legislation, frustrating bureaucracy and corruption, continue to make doing business difficult and unnecessarily costly for many firms. Other concerns include limitations on work permits for foreign managers and technical staff, as well as harassment by local and national "financial police" and other taxation authorities through intrusive inspections. Most investors therefore employ a large staff of attorneys, accountants, and invest significant resources to protect their interests. Foreign investors are also advised to pursue a long-time strategy and careful marketing approach to succeed in Kazakhstan's market.

Most of country's population is concentrated in either the southeast region of the country in cities such as Almaty, Southern Kazakhstan, and Zhambyl Oblasts, or the northern/northeast in the cities of Akmola, Karaganda, Kustanai, northern Kazakhstan, Pavlodar, and eastern Kazakhstan oblasts. These areas also have higher average incomes than in other parts of the

Table 5.3 Business Procedural Ranking – Kazakhstan

Ease of...	2006 rank	2005 rank	Change in rank
Doing business	63	82	+19
Starting a business	40	37	−3
Dealing with licenses	119	121	+2
Employing workers	22	21	−1
Registering property	76	81	+5
Getting credit	48	117	+69
Protecting investors	46	43	−3
Paying taxes	66	63	−3
Trading across borders	172	171	−1
Enforcing contracts	27	27	0
Closing a business	100	102	+2

Source: The World Bank, <www.doingbusiness.org/ExploreEconomies>.

Table 5.4   Kazakhstan – Singapore Joint Venture Case Study

Company shareholders: National Innovation Fund, Kazakhstan's Glotur Co. and Singapore's Das Multimedia

Date of establishment: February 2006

Start-up capital: $10 million

Main business: Manufacture of liquid-crystal computer monitors and plasma televisions.

Company developments:

With the help of the Innovation Fund, whose goal is to stimulate the development of the high-tech industries, a manufacturing center will be established at the Alatau IT City outside of Almaty.

Kazakh workers will assemble television monitors from Singapore supplied parts. Sixty percent of components for new products will be made locally.

The JV's officers explain that they entered the agreement as a result of Kazakhstan's competitive labor costs.

---

country. Additionally, the cities of Aktau, Uralsk and Atyrau in particular (considered the nation's oil capital) also boast expanding economies in the oil-rich western regions of the country where major international oil companies currently operate.

BANKING

Kazakhstan's banking sector is well run and considered one of the most developed in Central Asia. The National Bank and the Financial Supervision Agency supervise the banking system and have overseen a steady consolidation and strengthening of the system. In June 2005 the President signed the law "On Currency Regulation and Currency Control," lifting restrictions on money transfers to both residents and non-residents, who can withdraw up to $10,000 in cash out of the country without documentation of the money's origin. The National Bank has pursued market-based policies that have contributed to financial sector development. There is no distinction made between residents and non-residents when opening bank accounts, though the bank regularly monitors currency operations of selected non-residents and permits non-residents to pay wages in foreign currency. There are however restrictions on capital movements when a non-resident sells or disposes of an interest in a resident company to another resident company. Foreign investors seeking credit from local banks have often found margins required for credit to be burdensome; it is usually cheaper and simpler therefore to use retained earnings or borrow from their home country. Since 1998 Kazakhstan's banks have placed Eurobonds on international markets and obtained syndicated loans. The proceeds of which have been used to support domestic lending. Most major banks have been able to obtain reasonably good ratings from international credit assessment agencies, while by 2007 all are supposed to meet Basel I risk-weighted capital standards.

The Kazakhstan National Securities Commission has been operating since 1996 in compliance with the norms of the International Organization of Securities Commissioners. The Commission was made a department of the National Bank, and renamed the "Securities Market Regulation Department" in 2001. Two years later, the Department's main functions were given to a newly-created Financial Supervision Agency (FSA). The FSA has broad authority over the banking insurance sectors, as well as the stock market. The FSA is financed from the National Bank's budget and subordinated to the President of the RK.

Following a decade of consolidation which weeded out more than 150 banks, there are currently 34 banks in Kazakhstan. A robust local stock exchange, regional standards, and the full convertibility of the Kazakh currency, has helped the sector significantly. In addition, the relative strength in the region of Kazakhstan's financial laws and recent regulatory improvements have also helped the nation's banking sector. According to Lord Renwick, vice chairman of investment banking for JP Morgan Europe and vice chairman of JP Morgan Cazenove (February 2007), "there are three or four banks which have very good standards by international standards. And that is why the IPOs of, for instance, Kazkommertsbank and Halyk Bank, have been very successful to date." Renwick added that Bank TuranAlem is in the same category, and that if the firm comes to the market next year, TuranAlem will be "a very successful IPO."

CURRENCY

The Kazakhstan National Bank allows the tenge to float, and it is fully convertible with the US dollar. In 1996 Kazakhstan joined Article 8 of the International Monetary Fund Charter calling for full convertibility and the removal of controls on current account transactions. All incoming and outgoing transfers initiated in foreign currency are subject to currency controls imposed by the National Bank. Foreign currency transfers require supporting documentation (e.g. a copy of an invoice or a copy of a contract) justifying the purpose of the transfer, and can only be initiated from a foreign currency account. The following currency transactions are subject to currency control imposed by the National Bank under the Law on Currency Regulations: outgoing transfers in foreign currency (with the exception of business to government payments) initiated by residents to non-residents; by non-residents to residents; or by non-residents to non-residents.

The primary tool used in the framework of Kazakhstan's currency control system is "The Passport of Transactions," a cross-agency document filled out by the exporter/importer and reviewed by customs officials and representatives of the exporter/importer's bank. All transfers of funds can be executed by banks only after completion and approval of the passport of transaction.

Kazakhstan adopted Article 8 of the IMF Articles of Agreement in 1996 which stipulates that current account transactions will not be restricted. Three years later the government and National Bank of Kazakhstan announced that the national currency would be allowed to freely float at market rates. There are therefore minimal restrictions in Kazakhstan for conversion or transferring of funds associated with an investment into a freely usable currency at a legal market-clearing rate.

FOREIGN DIRECT INVESTMENT

The lion's share of foreign direct investment in to Kazakhstan has been as a result of its oil and mineral resources. The United States was the largest investing country in Kazakhstan in 2005 with $11.5 billion, followed by the Netherlands ($4.5 billion), the United Kingdom ($4.3 billion), and Italy ($2.4 billion). The largest single investment is TengizChevrOil (TCO), a joint-venture consortium between Chevron Overseas Petroleum Inc, Exxon Mobil, Kazakhstan's national oil and gas company (KazMunaiGaz), and LUKArco. This TCO investment is part of a 40-year, $20 billion agreement signed in 1993.

Kazakhstan has membership to the Eurasian Economic Community (EAEC) along with Russia, the Kyrgyz Republic, Belarus and Tajikistan. The EAEC is a successor to the Customs Union and is intended to harmonize trade tariffs and create a Eurasian free-trade zone. In addition, it is a member of the Central Asian Cooperation Organization.

TAXATION AND CUSTOMS

Kazakhstan's tax code has been streamlined and is fairly straightforward on paper. However, the tax regime falls short at the implementation stage, and tax administration has a poor collection record, added to which the large shadow economy represents a significant loss of potential revenue. Foreign companies are placed under strict scrutiny, while an increased taxation burden and the risks that the government's actions cause have resulted in unease among some foreign investors.

Kazakhstan's customs valuation rules largely conform to the WTO Valuation Agreement, though unfortunately the Kazakh 2003 customs code remains overly complicated and does not encourage transparency or the expeditious movement of goods. All goods entering customs territory of Kazakhstan must be declared within 30 days of their arrival to Kazakhstan, and receive customs approved at clearance points. A brief declaration and notification on arrival of goods must be submitted to the customs body within 24 hours after the goods cross the border and are placed in a temporary storage warehouse. A customs declaration must be filed by a Kazakhstan citizen. Foreign entities cannot deal directly with customs officials in Kazakhstan and must use services provided by licensed customs brokers having the right to operate in Kazakhstan. A declaration can be declared by a business organization registered under Kazakhstan law, or its affiliate or representative located in Kazakhstan, an individual entrepreneur registered in Kazakhstan, or a permanent resident of Kazakhstan. Private persons permitted to transfer goods under a simplified procedure are the exception to the rule.

To declare commercial goods at a Kazakh customs office for their release one must submit the paper and electronic copies of customs declarations and all other accompanying documents. Customs Cargo Declaration, of which five copies are required, must be completed in either Kazakh or Russian, while other documents may be submitted in English. Customs officers may however request a translation of such documents and notarization of the translation. A party declaring goods must also submit a set of the following: invoices, a contract for the supply of goods, an import/export transaction passport, and shipping documents.

A number of goods imported temporarily receive a full or partial waiver on customs duties and taxes such as transport vehicles, professional equipment, goods imported for demonstration purposes, shipping containers, and advertising materials. The period for temporary use may not exceed two years from the date of shipment. Documents must be submitted in such cases which specify the description and value of the goods, and a written confirmation stating that the goods will be sent out of Kazakhstan after a defined period. Raw materials, food-stuffs, and industrial wastes are not eligible for such exemptions even if they are intended for temporary use in Kazakhstan. Additionally, exemption from customs duties applies to certain equipment and components imported for the purpose of implementing investment projects in priority economy sectors, assuming such equipment is not available locally.

TRADE BARRIERS

An unwieldy government bureaucracy, lack of an effective judicial process for breach-of-contract resolution, and logistical difficulties serving the Kazakhstan market are some of the main trade barriers in the country. Service barriers are also problematic for investors. Under a 2000 law on insurance, overall charter capital of all foreign insurance companies should not exceed 25 percent in the non-life insurance market and 50 percent in the life insurance market. Foreign insurance firms as well as banks can operate only through a Kazakh entity, while foreigners in other industry sectors can operate through joint ventures with Kazakhstani companies or as a foreign company. Oil companies may purchase services only from Kazakhstani-based companies if they are available locally.

Export control laws in Kazakhstan are still in the early stages of development, though the government is currently working to improve rules on military and dual-use technology as well as sensitive and strategic materials. Export licenses are issued by the Ministry of Economy's Export Control Administration in cooperation with other relevant ministries.

Other documents may be required, depending on the nature of goods or circumstances of importation/exportation. These include: an import license, certificate of origin, certificate of conformity, power of attorney for customs processing, customs valuation declaration, packing list, insurance documents, statement of sanitary inspection, statistic card, and company registration certificate.

FREE/SPECIAL ECONOMIC ZONES

The EAEC (the Eurasian Economic Community) was established in 2000 in order to harmonize customs duties and promote free trade between the partners, and as a successor to an unsuccessful customs union between Kazakhstan, Russia, Belarus, Kyrgyzstan, and Tajikistan. The EAEC has made little progress in creating a free trade zone, as had been the case with the now defunct Customs Union. The importation of goods from EAEC free-trade partners and certain developing or less-developed countries is permitted into Kazakhstan free of duty or at a reduced rate within the framework of the Generalized System of Preferences.

Special Economic Zones (SEZs) were established in 2001 in the capital city of Astana and in 2002 on the territory of the seaport of Aktau by the Kazakh government. A third SEZ has been established near the city of Shymkent as an incubator for the cotton textile industry under the "cluster" strategy, where the state attempts to create new industrial sectors where it has identified the potential for the growth of competitive firms. There are plans to build clusters in the petrochemical, oil machinery, food processing, tourism, transport and metallurgical sectors as well. "Technoparks" are also examples of areas where investors can take advantage of incentives to develop trade-intensive high-tech industries.

LABOR

Despite the fact that Kazakhstan has an educated and technically competent workforce, finding a professional English-speaking labor pool can sometimes be difficult with the exception of Almaty. Additionally, training is usually considered essential to opening a business in Kazakhstan. Pay scales, like other former Soviet republics, tend to reward age and seniority rather than ability.

In 1998, the government introduced an accumulation pension system that requires all employed persons to contribute 10 percent of their salary to accumulation pension funds. One year later, the nation's 1999 Labor Law and the Constitution guaranteed basic workers' rights, including the right to organize and the right to strike. In general, Kazakhstan's labor regulations tend to be tilted towards the employee and impose a heavy burden on businesses. Occasional strikes have occurred, usually for short periods. Trade unions remain weak and poorly organized, while strikes, if they do occur, tend to be linked to failed restructuring in the state sector and broader economic conditions.

The 1996 Law on Labor Disputes and Strikes restricts strikes by requiring that a peaceful attempt at a solution first be made, that two-thirds of the labor collective must approve the strike, and that the employer must be warned 15 days in advance in writing, among other restrictions. In addition, strikes for political purposes are forbidden. The 1993 Law on Professional Labor Unions provides a legal guarantee against limitations of labor and grants social – economic, political and personal rights and freedoms as a result of membership in a union. That same year Kazakhstan joined the International Labor Organization (ILO). Since then it has ratified 16 ILO conventions, including those pertaining to minimum employment age, forced labor, discrimination in employment, equal remuneration, and collective bargaining. Respect for trade union rights is strong, though the government does not hesitate to use the police and, on occasion, violence against strikers. The potential for labor unrest exists in the event of an economic downturn in Latvia, though industrial disputes are generally peaceful.

The Government of Kazakhstan has made it a priority to ensure that Kazakhstani citizens are well-represented on foreign enterprise workforces, especially at managerial and executive ranks. There is also increased pressure to hire local labor through the introduction of requirements to search for local workers prior to the issuance of work permits for foreign labor. Foreign workers are required to have a work permit to work legally in Kazakhstan, a process which can at times be difficult and expensive.

MARKETING GOODS AND SERVICES

ESTABLISHING A BUSINESS

A company wishing to operate with a physical presence in Kazakhstan must first register with local authorities. Relevant documents, including an application for registration, by-laws of the entity to be registered, and by-laws of the foreign partner of the joint venture, should be submitted to the local department of the Ministry of Justice, which then sends the documentation to all other committees and offices. The process, which also requires of fee of around $500, should take no more than two to three weeks, though government computer malfunctions and other unexpected delays do occur on occasion. It is advisable to employ reputable and well-established legal counsel when registering a company.

The most common type of business is a branch office, limited liability partnership, or joint-stock company. There are an estimated 4,000 joint ventures registered in Kazakhstan. Joint ventures can be organized as a limited liability partnership or a joint stock company. A joint venture may be required when dealing with a privatization deal. A large number of joint ventures operate in Kazakhstan's energy sector, one of the largest being the TengizChevroil between state-owned KazMunayGas and Chevron. Kazakhstan's oil rich Atyrau oblast region has some 300 joint ventures alone, with partners from 55 countries. Other sectors which have may joint ventures are mining, agribusiness, transportation and food processing.

Despite the low population density of the country, some industry observers maintain that franchises have significant potential for development in Kazakhstan. Although the concept of franchising is relatively new in the country, a growing number of investors are viewing it as a potentially lucrative option. However, a lack of offers from franchises interested in the Kazakhstan market has also slowed franchise expansion. Local observers feel that significant short-term potential exists for franchises in food processing, especially in areas of the country being developed by foreign oil companies. Potentially lucrative opportunities exists in the areas of fast food and coffee shops, hotels and motels, auto parts/services, hypermarkets, ready-to-wear, computer/technical services, printing services, cleaning/laundry, fitness centers, and spas. Since judges in Kazakhstan are not familiar with franchise

Table 5.5   Doing Business in Kazakhstan

Indicator	Kazakhstan	Region	OECD
Number of procedures	7	9.4	6.2
Number of days	20	32	16.6
Cost (percent of income per capita)	7	14.1	5.3
Minimum Capital (percent of income per capita)	23.1	53.9	36.1

Source: The World Bank, <www.doingbusiness.org/ExploreEconomies>.

law, it is advisable to carefully draft any contract pertaining to such an operation.

Finding a reliable partner in Kazakhstan is an important step which will require time and effort, due diligence, and caution. Foreign investors should verify the reliability and reputation of a potential trade partner, as well as their achievements. It is advisable that one also verify all trade references, and check banking records and correspondent account capability with western banks.

DISTRIBUTION CHANNELS

Foreign firms must offer its customers in Kazakhstan convenient customer support and a reliable supply of products to their distributors. As a result of the country's vast size, equivalent in area to all of Eastern Europe, distribution networks must also be reliable.

Kazakhstan's distribution and telecommunications networks have been upgraded in recent years. A combination of marketing methods is suggested. These can include distributing or direct sales, working through a country-wide distributor or agent, working through more than one local-area distributor or agent, and/or distributing or selling products directly from a warehouse. Keep in mind that distribution channels still require extensive training, service support, and project financing such as leasing schemes for equipment.

Furthermore, it is advisable that one consider establishing a business in one of Kazakhstan's major urban centers, as they have the largest populations and are the best connection via transportation systems, offering investors the greatest potential market for consumer products.

PROMOTION AND ADVERTISING

Numerous local as well as western advertising firms operate in Kazakhstan, mainly in Almaty. Primary advertising channels for consumer goods are television, outdoor advertising, and general-interest publications. Image promotion and advertising of services is usually done using outdoor advertising and personal sales. Some other forms of direct marketing which are becoming increasingly popular are the distribution of free samples at points of sale and major cultural events, and marketing by mail.

Kazakhstan's Law on Advertising of 2003 and the Law Concerning Mass Media regulates the advertising industry. Under the law, advertising alcoholic products, baby formula, and products not licensed in the country, is prohibited. Advertising tobacco is permitted only in printed publications, so long as they are not on the first or last page of the publication. All advertised products should be certified. Permission for the advertisement of medicines and medical products is given by the Ministry of Health. Radio and television advertisements cannot occupy more than 15 percent of a broadcast, while it is forbidden to interrupt official statements, and appearances of presidential candidates.

News programs constitute up to one-third of total air time on Kazakhstan's airwaves. The most popular television channels are: Eurasia (countrywide), KTK (countrywide), Channel 31 (15 larger cities), and Khabar (countrywide), which is the country's leading national channel that broadcasts in Kazakh and Russian to over 13 million potential viewers. In addition, it is the only channel that organizes live transmissions of world sporting competitions.

In terms of printed material, some of the most popular weekly newspapers are *Panorama*, the English-language based newspaper *Almaty Herald*, *Central Asia Times*, and *Kazakhstan Monitor*. The most popular magazine for advertising is *Cosmopolitan-Kazakhstan* and the most popular radio channels are: "Russkoye Radio," "Europa+," and "Radio NS."

Exhibitions are also an increasingly popular way to gain clients in Kazakhstan. The exhibition industry has grown significantly in Almaty as well as other large cities such as Astana and Atyrau. The largest trade show is the annual Kazakhstan International Oil and Gas Exhibition (KIOGE). Other trade shows include the Food Expo, the Kazakhstan International Health Exhibition (KIHE), the Kazakhstan International Telecommunications Exhibition (KITEL), and a power and energy exhibition (KAZPOWER).

PRICING

Kazakhstan consumers are sensitive to prices and quality, and are generally willing to pay higher prices only for products with a recognizable name, or those justified with appropriate marketing or other special features such as uniqueness or higher quality. Relatively cheap products from Russia and

China are also an important part of the local market and a factor to take in to consideration when marketing lower-cost goods.

Transportation costs, import duties and certification payments must be taken into consideration when considering pricing. The overall trade-weighted import tariff is around 10 percent, though other factors represent more important issues for foreign investors. These include the fact that customs regulations tend to change and there can be large discrepancies between interpretations of such regulations in various parts of the country. In addition, the value-added tax to be paid on top of all customs duties and excise taxes at the time of customs clearance is also a major factor in terms of pricing. It is therefore advisable to work with customs brokers.

Local companies in Kazakhstan are extremely sensitive to pricing and contract financing terms. Since risk of nonpayment always exists, it is advisable to balance sales opportunities with such risk where entering the market, as well as beginning transactions on a full prepayment basis when possible. Project financing will also increase the likelihood and potential amount of transactions.

LEGAL REVIEW

JUDICIARY

Kazakhstan's judicial system is still in the process of being developed. As a result, court performance is often less than optimal. Kazakhstan's weak judiciary greatly complicates the process of doing business, while new oil and gas procurement laws tend to favor local suppliers and mandate extensive government interference in the procurement process. The legal system remains under the influence of the executive in disputes and does not generally uphold the interests of foreign investors; in some cases, the government has even encouraged the courts to assist local investors in their confiscation of foreign investors' property. In such cases, however, several foreign investors have obtained redress in foreign courts.

A great many other concerns center on legal innovations and changes to contracts that mitigate the current risk of investing in Kazakhstan and threaten to erode investor rights. The judicial process is slow and standards are low. Interpretation of laws by the central government often varies from in-terpretations of local officials. This is especially true in regard to implementation of Kazakhstan's system of taxation and collection of revenues.

Kazakhstan's Civil Code establishes general commercial law principles, while the general Provisions of the Civil Code were adopted in 1994 and have been amended several times since. Specific Provisions were passed by the

Parliament in 1999. Since commercial law development is still currently underway, retaining strong legal counsel is extremely advisable for understanding Kazakhstan's challenging market. In addition to ongoing changes in commercial law, enforcement of judgment also poses significant problems, and a judicial enforcement system is only beginning to be established by the Ministry of Justice. In addition, contradictory norms hinder the functioning of the legal system. Under the 2003 law "On Investments," contracts signed subsequent to its enactment may be subject to amendments in domestic legislation and international treaty provisions that change "the procedure and conditions of the import, manufacture, and sale of goods subject to excise duties." The law on foreign investment removing "grandfather rights" or protection from legislative changes after a contract has been signed has increased the risks to foreign investors since the right to international arbitration has been eliminated from the investment laws. The country's institutional governance is weak, further adding to the problems of transparency in commercial transactions, while government officials have a large say in many transactions, regardless of their size.

INTELLECTUAL PROPERTY

The protection of intellectual property rights is improving, though pirated products are still readily available. Patent protection is available for inventions, industrial designs and prototypes, though patent protection for certain types of products and processes including layout designs and plant variety has yet to be made available in Kazakhstan.

Patents are granted for a period of 20 years for inventions, while industrial designs are granted on a five-year basis. Prototypes are granted a five-year initial period of protection, with the possibility of an additional three-year extension. Currently, discrepancies exist in fees charged to domestic patent and trademark applicants, as compared to foreign applicants.

Trademark violation is a crime in Kazakhstan, despite the fact that enforcement of the rule is not always consistent. However, amendments to the Administrative, Criminal and Civil Procedural Codes have been adopted to bolster enforcement capabilities.

Kazakhstan's 1996 Law on Copyrights and Related Rights is largely in conformity with the requirements of the WTO TRIPS Agreement and the Berne Convention, which was ratified in 1998, and the Geneva Phonograms Convention in 2000.

LICENSING

Kazakhstan intends to streamline its licensing rules, though the government has not yet approved most of the qualification and procedural requirements for issuing licenses. As a result, some businesses have been left vulnerable to inspection bodies, which have threatened them with fines and shutdowns for not having licenses that are, in many instances, impossible to legally obtain. The high number of licenses required for most activities is also an obstacle to business. Despite the fact that the Kazakh government has removed the need for import and export licenses on most commodities, procedures on the remaining products, which are often slow and lacking transparency and therefore costly, remain a major obstacle to investment and trade in Kazakhstan. Under the 1995 Law on Licensing, many economic activities such as healthcare services, notary services, telecommunications services, and juridical services are subject to licensing regulations, and there is an extensive list of goods that are subject to this requirement in cases of import or transit through the territory of Kazakhstan. In addition, pesticides, medicine, drugs, nuclear materials, weapons, certain chemicals, and industrial waste, canned meat, chicken, sausages, wine, and a number of other products are also subject to licensing requirements. Licenses must be issued within a one-month period, and for entities of small business, no later than ten days from the date of submission of the application with all required documents (unless another deadline is established by legislative acts).

Additional challenges are posed to importers into Kazakhstan by the 1999 Law on Certification. International Certificates of Quality cannot replace Kazakhstani Certificates of Conformity and can only serve as a reference for the local certification agency. Certification procedures might take up to two months in cases of import operations. Gosstandart is the Committee on Technical Regulation and Metrology and the national body regulating standardization, certification, and conformity assessment issues in Kazakhstan. Third-country certificates are not accepted in Kazakhstan. However, such certificates have been known to expedite the process of acquiring Kazakhstani certificates. Customs brokers or professional service providers can also be helpful in arranging such matters. Several amendments to the Licensing Law were passed in the first half of 2005, excluding a variety of business activity from licensing requirements, including aircraft repair, airport services, sale of topographic and geodesic maps, excursion and tourist business, and legal services (excluding advocacy).

STANDARDIZATION

Beginning in 2000, Kazakhstan banned the sale of certain products not labeled in both Kazakh and Russian, though some products, such as pharmaceuticals, were exempted from the dual language requirement. Unfortunately, government observance of standards, testing, labeling, and certification requirements suffers from lack of uniformity and has constituted a major barrier to investors when they differ significantly from internationally accepted standards.

A new law "On Technical Regulation" was adopted in 2004, as certification and conformity are part of the national system of technical regulation. Since Kazakhstan strongly wishes to join the WTO, it has strived to harmonize its legal base with international standards. Kazakhstan was the sixth country in the CIS to adopt an internationally accepted model of technical regulation. Under the new legislation, authorities can initiate other reforms in the system of technical regulation, which will last until 2010.

Although Kazakhstan is a member of the ISO, it does not have full membership in the international organizations dealing with accreditation (ILAC and IAF). Currently, mechanisms for international standard adoption are in place. Implementation of a number of international standards in Kazakhstan is extremely problematic due to legal and technical inconsistencies. Consequently, frustrating procedures for standardization include state control over conformity with mandatory standard requirements, mandatory certification and examination, and registration.

BUSINESS ETHICS

Corruption is widely perceived to be prevalent throughout Kazakhstan despite the country's Criminal Code containing special penalties for such acts. Foreign investors have cited corruption as a significant obstacle to investment in Kazakhstan. Additionally, law enforcement agencies have on occasion brought pressure on foreign investors perceived to be uncooperative with the government.

In order to combat corruption, the Ministry of Interior, the Financial Police and the Committee for National Security (KNB) were established, while the Disciplinary State Service Commission was also established in June 2003.

INVESTMENT OPPORTUNITIES

MINING INDUSTRY

Due to its richness of resources, including coal, and ferrous and non-ferrous metals, Kazakhstan has a large mining industry that accounts for more than one-third of the nation's export earnings and 15 percent of its GDP. There are over 200 separate enterprises which produce or process a significant number of substances including coal, iron and steel, copper, lead, zinc, manganese, gold, aluminum, titanium sponge, uranium, and barites.

Despite the sector's important role in the economy of the nation and whole regions within it, much of the technology and management practices of the mining industry are outdated and date from the Soviet times, a fact which has hampered the sale of mining companies to foreign firms. Currently, most of its mining equipment comes from Russia. In the mid-1990s many new firms entered the market and invested in exploration and development. However, nearly all ended up leaving the country, complaining of significant lack of transparency and arbitrary and confusing laws which favored local businesses.

Consequently, more than half of Kazakhstani mining, processing, and smelting enterprises use outdated equipment that is often in need of repair, while nearly all lack environmentally friendly technologies. Trade opportunities may exist for foreign firms in used and refurbished equipment, as well as in turnkey project management.

ENVIRONMENTAL GOODS AND SERVICES

There is strong potential demand for western environmental solutions in Kazakhstan as a result of the country's high concentration of natural resource-based industries due to its growing oil extraction operations, as well as its weak and poorly enforced environmental laws. Such a need is sure to grow as Kazakhstan's economy expands and its citizens become more environmentally aware.

Kazakhstan's government expenditures on environmental protection are among the lowest in Eurasia, comprising only $0.50 per person per year, since few enterprises can afford the installation of air and water pollution control systems. Meanwhile, when new equipment is purchased, it is normally technically lacking. However, in an effort to begin managing this increasingly acute issue, a program is being developed by Kazakhstan's Ministry of Environment to get the problem under control by 2010.

Kazakhstan's environmental consulting market is expanding as the need and ability to implement such projects – due to the funding of international development firms such as the World Bank – becomes greater. It is advisable to keep track of major projects financed by multilateral development banks, and to work jointly with Kazakhstani environmental organizations as environmental consulting services.

Cleaner drinking water, primary and secondary wastewater treatment, air pollution control, and environmentally friendly technologies for oil extraction and transportation are considered the most pressing issues for Kazakhstan currently, and have therefore attracted the most attention of international development institutions. The most promising sub-sectors include: industrial water and air filters, urban water sanitation systems, water treatment/analysis equipment, solid waste recycling equipment, equipment for soil remediation and oil spill cleanup, equipment for municipal waste processing, and technologies for hazardous waste collection, disposal, and treatment.

OIL AND GAS INDUSTRIES

Kazakhstan has more than 2 percent of the world's proven oil reserves, with potential reserves of over 90 billion barrels, ranking it within the world's top ten oil provinces. It is the second largest oil producer among the former Soviet Republics after Russia, producing nearly 1.3 million barrels per day (bpd), expected to reach more than two million barrels of oil per day by 2010, and over 3.5 million barrels per day by 2015. The Kazakhstani government is planning for oil production to reach about 2.7 billion bpd by 2020. The magnitude of the resource could result in Kazakhstan becoming one of the world's major energy exporters by the end of the decade.

Consequently, investors continue to focus heavily on the hydrocarbons sector. The Kazakhstan Ministry of Energy is looking at scenarios for a number of pipeline routes to handle this export surge. Industry experts estimate that the current market for oil and gas field equipment and services will grow some 15–30 percent annually over the next three years.

Kazakhstan's natural gas reserves, on the other hand, are estimated at 5.9 trillion cubic meters (tcm). However, insufficient branching of developed trunk gas pipelines, and significant amount of modernization needed on existing networks, limits the amount of local natural gas consumed. As a result, natural gas imports remain considerable, especially in the south and southeastern regions.

Opportunities for foreign investors exist in nearly all sub-sectors associated with oil extraction, processing and transportation, especially geological exploration, geophysics, hydrogeology, drilling, research and data management, laboratory studies, oil spill cleanup technologies, and pipeline equipment and services.

In 2003, the Government of Kazakhstan approved a development program for oil fields in the Caspian Sea, calling for increasing offshore oil production in the Caspian to about 2.0 million bpd by 2015, and for development of terrestrial infrastructure. Until then, the government expects 51 billion dollars to be invested into the development of the country's oil and gas sector. In addition, plans to put more than one hundred offshore blocks up for tender exist. Furthermore, Kazakhstan as yet has no experience in offshore production and operations, a fact that can translate into investment opportunities in rig work, support infrastructure, and environmentally sensitive technologies. The sector also presents opportunities for investment in oil extraction, processing, engineering and construction, transportation, and storage, particularly in oil tools (completion, work-over, and services), well stimulation, water injection and gas treatment packages, support infrastructure, and environmental technologies. The most promising sub sectors, meanwhile, are offshore/onshore oil and gas drilling and production equipment; turbines, compressors and pumps for pipeline applications; measurement and process control equipment for pipeline applications; industrial automation, control and monitoring systems for refineries, gas processing and petrochemical plants, seismic processing and interpretation, petroleum software development, sulfur removal and disposal technologies, well stimulation and field abandonment services.

POWER GENERATION

Some two-thirds of Kazakhstan's electricity production is generated at coalfired plants, while the rest is from petroleum-fired plants and seven hydroelectric stations. Most of Kazakhstan's Regional Electric Companies (RECs), which ensure distributions of energy, have yet to be privatized. Most RECs are in poor condition and require major repairs and replacements. Electricity transmission networks are extremely inefficient, with losses estimated at 15 percent or more during transmission and distribution. Major investment opportunities, therefore, will arise as the privatization process moves forward. Construction of new power plants and expansion of power distribution networks is being considered.

Kazakhstan's Ministry of Energy estimates that from 2006 to 2010, the sector will need around $4 billion, and $4.5 million from 2011–15. New production facilities are needed, while old ones need to be modernized. The program to upgrade the country's power grid networks will cost an estimated $258.4 million, of which $73.4 million will come from the funds of KEGOC (the state-owned Kazakhstan Electricity Grid Operating Company), with $140 million coming from the World Bank, and $45 million from the European Bank for Reconstruction and Development.

Industry observers predict that Kazakhstan's power generation sector will boost its total capacity to 86 billion kWh by 2015, while power consumption at that time is projected to reach 81 billion kWh. Current government economic development plans call for the upgrade of power facilities, the launch of a North – South power transmission line, and the construction of small hydropower plants.

Goods currently imported by the electric power generation sector include non-irradiated fuel elements, liquid dielectric transformers, inverters, parts for transformers and inverters, and vapor generating boilers and parts. In addition, experts predict that as management and communications systems grow, so too will the need for IT support. Furthermore, the ability of foreign investors to supply equipment to Kazakhstan to secure project financing can be a decisive factor allowing increased profitability and market share.

MEDICAL EQUIPMENT

Kazakhstan's demand for medical equipment is expected to increase due to the sustained growth of the national economy and increased health-care spending. There is currently a need to replace some 80 percent of the sector's equipment, considered obsolete.

The Kazakhstan government recently adopted a new program for reformation and development of the health-care sector, which accounts for nearly 3 percent of overall GDP. The 1.3 billion USD program, set to run through 2010, envisions increasing state health-care expenditures to up to 4 percent of GDP by 2008 by reforming and developing the country's primary health-care networks, improving the public health administration system, providing enhanced medical personnel training, improving mother and child health services, and emphasizing preventive measures such as diagnostics, treatment of social diseases, and patient rehabilitation.

Most procurement for public health-care institutions in Kazakhstan is done through government-organized tenders in a process generally lacking transparency. National procurement legislation stipulates that small companies registered in Kazakhstan have a preference over others in such a tender process.

Currently, nearly all medical equipment in Kazakhstan is imported, with such imports increasing substantially on an annual basis. The market is especially receptive to western medical equipment of high quality. There are about 10–15 well-established, reliable importers of medical equipment most of whose wholesale distributors are located in Almaty or Astana. Industry observers maintain that opportunities for investment exist in electro-medical diagnostic and therapy equipment, diagnostic imaging with a special emphasis on X-ray equipment and supplies, surgical supplies, dental equipment and supplies, test kits and laboratory equipment.

AGRICULTURE

Nearly one-tenth of the value of Kazakhstan's economic production is derived from agriculture. Arable land makes up some 12 percent of the country's total territory, or 30 million hectares with wheat, barley, cotton, and rice being the major crops. Wheat accounts for some $300–400 million in exports annually, and is one of the country's leading export commodities. Sheep and cattle are raised throughout the country, and chief livestock products are dairy, leather, wool and meat.

The major demand for grain harvesting combines, wheel tractors, sprayers and grain-cleaning equipment is currently satisfied by imports, though the Kazakhstan government is seeking ways of production of such products locally. A 2003 Land Code limits foreign ownership of land in Kazakhstan to a maximum of a 10-year lease. However, foreigners can invest in agricultural production and gain control of land through a locally registered firm.

Agricultural producers have accumulated financial resources and are actively using them to replace or modernize outdated machinery, which accounts for some 80 percent of all machinery in use. Major investments have been made by agricultural companies in recent years into grain harvesting combines, tractors, equipment for poultry and egg production, grain drying and cleaning equipment, and milk drawing equipment. There is limited local production of such items, as well as limited production of plows, seeders, mowers and reapers.

Investment opportunities for both new and used products lie in pneumatic seeders, reapers, sprayers, grain drying and cleaning technologies, and storage quality control systems, as well as 100–150 hp tractors and combines for southern regions and the larger than 250 hp tractors for northern regions. Investors in this sector are advised to closely follow developments if reform plans implemented by the government on the agricultural sector.

FOOD PROCESSING AND PACKAGING MACHINERY

The Kazakhstani food processing and packaging machinery sector has demonstrated significant growth in recent years. The government recently subsidized a program for the development of the leasing of food processing machinery, and another for decreased interest rates at commercial banks for food processing companies.

Domestic production of food processing and packaging equipment is extremely limited and therefore almost entirely represented by imported equipment, with Russia, Turkey, China, Italy, and Germany being major sources. Major market segments include grain processing, meat and poultry, dairy products, alcoholic and non-alcoholic beverages, breweries, vegetable oil and fats, sugar and confectionery, tobacco products, processing of soy beans, packaging materials, and glass and paper packaging.

The fish processing sub-sector is expected to develop in the coming years, especially since the Kazakhstan government has obliged international oil firms operating in the Caspian Sea to invest in local fishing in compensation for harming bio-resources. The diversification of fish processing, launching new productions such as fish-skin processing, artificial breeding of sturgeon on plots of the coast for further caviar production, production of oil for the perfume industry, and manufacturing of long-shelf life preserves, are all expected to develop as part of this process. In addition, traditional fish processing is limited and it is expected that there will be new processing facilities installed for the production of finished products such as dried and smoked fish, fish fillet, and freshly frozen fish.

Meat and dairy processing industries are also expected to develop, as the cattle breeding industry has shown signs of coming out of recession. As the cattle breeding industry develops in Kazakhstan, more dairy and meat processing equipment will be required. Best prospects include equipment for deep processing of grain, especially ethanol and gluten, vegetables and fruit processing, the production of natural juices and canned products, vegetable oil, ready-to-finish products for supermarkets, production of soy-based products, snacks, processing of meat/poultry, milk and fish, packaging equipment and materials, and small capacity laboratory testing equipment for milk and dairy processing industries.

BUILDING INDUSTRY

As infrastructure plans and urban and commercial expansion continue, the Kazakh building industry will continue to grow rapidly. Many opportunities exist in Astana, and in strengthening and diversifying the country's infrastructure. Plans are also underway for upgrading, expanding or building new ports, airports, roads, and power distribution grids. In addition, as investment expands, there is demand for worker housing commercial structures, and improved site infrastructure. The demand for building equipment and materials has also expanded as a result, growing at an average annual rate of 30 percent over the past several years. The building industry, on the other hand, has grown by more than 20 percent per year.

Construction companies, including international ones, also have found prospects for investment in Kazakhstan since 1997, when the rebuilding of Astana began. The demand for machinery, construction equipment and materials, has increased as a result. There still remains a need for modern offices, housing and a highway system in the growing city. One of the fastest growing sectors of the market is for high quality materials used in the finishing and renovation process, including wall & floor coverings, ceiling products, doors and windows, kitchen and bath equipment, plumbing and electrical equipment, and hardware.

There are also several infrastructure projects, including a new oil port in Aktau, directed at the needs of the oil industry, upon which the construction sector is largely dependent. There has been increased need for banks, hotels, housing and other buildings. There is also a need for the full range of civil engineering, construction, and engineering activities.

Less than half of the construction materials used in Kazakhstan are available domestically, while the rest are imported from Turkey, China, and Germany. Although items such as the following are in fact produced locally, they are generally not considered to meet international quality: cement, bricks, wooden doors, windows, steel doors, and soft and iron roofs. However, domestic production of a number of new quality and cost competitive basic products has been established, such as: fiberglass insulation materials, roofing and waterproofing products, energy efficient glass, aluminum extrusion, engineering equipment, cement, bricks, and wall panels.

TELECOMMUNICATIONS

Kazakhstan's Information and Communications Technologies (ICT) has been marked as an important strategic industry in need of modernization by government authorities, and has subsequently set forth a long-term modernization and liberalization plan. Key drivers of the national telecom sector include the deployment of a fiber-optic network across Kazakhstan, providing international connectivity, digitalization of exchanges surpassing 64 percent by the end of first quarter of 2005, adoption of a new law on telecommunications in July 2004, and liberalization of the market.

Mobile communications is the most rapidly developing segment of the communications market. The number of mobile phone subscribers in 2004 reached some 18 percent, surpassing the number of fixed-line subscribers. There are three mobile operators in Kazakhstan, including two GSM operators: GSM Kazakhstan (trademarks Kcell and Activ) with about 2 million subscribers, and KarTel (trademarks K-mobile, Excess, and Beeline) with 1.8 million subscribers, and one CDMA operator Altel (Dalacom and Pathword trademarks).

A relatively strong fixed-line penetration of around 15.9 telephone lines per 100 inhabitants exists in Kazakhstan, with six operators serving about 2.5 million subscribers. A growing demand exists for more telecom equipment and services for mobile, fixed line telephony, cable, broadband, value-added mobile systems, data services, and all types of internet-related communication services. The government plans to attract operators to provide universal services in the rural areas of Kazakhstan by deployment of CDMA-450 network, and installation of communication kiosks.

New telecommunications legislation adopted in June 2004 provides all operators equal access to the telecommunications network of Kazakhstan, introduces universal services to conform to practices in other countries, and brought in a system of alternative operators of international and long-distance services by abolishing the exclusive license of state-controlled telecommunications company, Kazakhtelecom,. However, the new rule still limits foreign ownership to 49 percent for operators of the ground fixed lines providing international and long-distance telephony services.

Aside from coaxial and fiber-optic cables, and small PBXs production, there is almost no domestic production of telecom equipment. Imports represent 98 percent of the telecommunications equipment market, while volumes of domestic production are far below demand of the market.

General Information

Communication Services

Domestic telephone service in Kazakhstan is generally poor despite recent and projected improvements. The main challenge for telecommunications is the nation's small population spread over a vast territory. International service is reliable in major cities despite being expensive. Both GSM and CDMA mobile technology are available in most cities throughout Kazakhstan.

Kazakhtelecom, the state-controlled telecommunications company, is actively building a fully-digital national telecommunications network based on digital local and long-distance switches and fiber-optic lines linking all major cities of the country. In addition, fiber optics and other communications lines are being laid in order to compete in a deregulated market.

A dozen companies provide dial-up and leased line (ADSL) internet access in cities throughout Kazakhstan, and dial-up internet service is generally available at any location with a phone connection. Broadband solutions are also available in major cities via cable or satellite. Fax machines and photocopiers are also available at major urban centers.

Local Customs

Kazakhstan business customs draw on a combination of Russian and Central Asian cultural influences. Most people shake hands (although men generally do not shake women's hands in company) and call people by their first names at business meetings.

Small gifts such as pens, company logo pins, memo, and books are often given at the end of an initial meeting as a token of appreciation.

Businessmen in Kazakhstan are generally less than direct, resulting in the need for a greater number of business meetings than in others countries as well as the need for patience on the part of some foreign investors.

Having dinner with business contacts after more formal business contacts have been established are common, along with after-hours informal meetings, dinners and toasts, as well as weekend hunting trips and barbecues.

Having a competent interpreter can also add invaluable context to your business meetings. Business attire is generally a suit and tie for men, and a suit or business dress for women, even at less formal dinner meetings.

Visas and Residency

Visas are absolutely necessary in Kazakhstan, and foreign visitors risk being deported if they do not have a valid visa. All travelers transiting Kazakhstan must obtain a Kazakhstani transit visa, which is valid for three days. All travelers must also register with the Kazakhstani Office of Visas and Registration (OVIR) within three days of arrival, as steep penalties will be imposed at the airport upon departure if the proper documentation from OVIR has not been obtained in advance.

In some cases local firms hosting a foreign visitor or even major hotels can help with such procedures. Otherwise, written request for registration, purpose of the trip and places in Kazakhstan to be visited and other information will need to be presented at the main Almaty OVIR office, a process which will generally take a full day. If the traveler was registered at the time of border passing, however, this registration is valid for three months.

Helpful Resources – Kazakhstan

Government Resources

CIS Interstate Council on Standardization, Metrology, and Certification: www.easc.org.by/
Ministry of Agriculture; Committee for Water Resources: www.minagri.kz
Ministry for Environmental Protection in Kazakhstan: www.nature.kz/
Ministry of Health and Associations: www.dari.kz

Trade Shows

KazExpo Service: www.kazexpo.kz
Atakent-Expo: www.exhibitions.kz
North Caspian Regional Oil & Gas Exhibition: http://caspianworld.com/en/go/
Kazakhstan International Oil & Gas Exhibition and Conference: www.kioge.com/home.html
Power Kazakhstan: http://caspianworld.com/
Kazakhstan International Health-care Exhibition: www.kihe.kz
BuildExpo Kazakhstan: www.tntexpo.com/buildk.html
Major Telecom Trade Show: www.kitel.kz
Customs Info: http://www.customs.kz

Miscellaneous

Khabar News Agency: www.khabar.kz
ITECA: www.iteca.kz
Kazakhstanskaya Pravda: www.kazpravda.kz
Novoye Pokoleniye: www.np.kz
Panorama: www.panorama.kz
Vremya: www.time.kz
Alma TV: www.almatv.kz
MiningWorld Central Asia: http://caspianworld.com/
Regional Environmental Centre for Central Asia: www.carec.kz/
Kazakhstan Business Association for Sustainable Development: www.kap.kz/
Kazakhstan Water Partnership: http://atasu.org
Medical news in Kazakhstan: www.pharmnews.kz
AgriTek Kazakhstan, Foodtek Kazakhstan, PackTek Kazakhstan: www.tntexpo.com

AgriTek Kazakhstan, Foodtek Kazakhstan, PackTek Kazakhstan:
www.tntexpo.com
Astana Food: www.iteca.kz
Atyrau Build: www.atyraubuild.kz/
Kaz Build: www.kazbuild.kz/
Agency on Informatization and Telecommunications of Kazakhstan:
    www.aic.gov.kz
Kazakhstan Online: http://www.online.kz
Nursat: www.nursat.kz
Astel: www.astel.kz
BankNet: www.banknet.kz
Kazakhtelecom: www.telecom.kz

Select Bibliography

Aaslund, Anders. "How Russia Became a Market Economy."
The Brookings Institution, Washington D.C., 1995.

Asel, Paul. "Reengineering Russia." MBA thesis, Stanford University –
Graduate School of Business, 1991.

Ayios, Angela. "Competence and trust guardians as key elements of building
trust in east–west joint ventures in Russia." *Business Ethics: A European
Review* 12 (2), 190–202, 2003.

Baker, Peter, and Glasser, Susan. *Kremlin Rising: Vladimir Putin's Russia and
the End of Revolution.* New York: Simon & Schuster, 2005

Barisitz, Stephan. "The Development of the Banking Sectors in Russia,
Ukraine, Belarus and Kazakhstan since Independence."
Oesterreichische National Bank, 2000.

Belew, Bill. "Joint Ventures in Russia – Budweiser." *Pan Asian Biz*, 26 June
2006.

The CIA Worldfactbook:
http://www.umsl.edu/services/govdocs/wofact2005

D'Anieri, Paul. J. *Economic Interdependence in Ukrainian – Russian Relations.*
Albany: State University of New York Press, 1999.

D'Anieri, Paul, Krawchuk, Robert, and Kuzio, Taras. *Politics and Society in
Ukraine.* Boulder: Westview, 1999.

Doing Business in Kazakhstan – McGuire Woods: www.mcguirewoods.com

The Economist Intelligence Unit – Country Reports, 2006, Country
Factbook for Latvia, Lithuania, Kazakhstan, Russia and Ukraine:
http://www.economist.com/countries

Ernst & Young: http://www.ey.com

"Doing Business in Lithuania. Tax Guide 2007."

"Kazakhstan Business Brief," 2006.

"Russia Compensation & Benefits Survey – Russia," 2006/2007.

"Ukraine Compensation & Benefits Survey 2006/2007."

"Foreign Direct Investment in the States of the Former USSR."

The World Bank Washington, D.C. 1992.

Hamill, Jim. "Joint Ventures in Russia The Experience of Two Small Companies." *Journal of East–West Business*, Volume 1, Issue 4, 1996.

Harasymiw, Bohdan. *Post-Communist Ukraine*. Edmonton and Toronto: Canadian Institute of Ukrainian Studies, 2002.

Herbig, Paul. "Ukraine: society in transition – cultural aspects," 1997.

Hirschhausen, Christian von. "New Neighbours in Eastern Europe: Economic and Industrial Reform in Lithuania, Latvia and Estonia," *Sciences économiques et sociales*, 1998.

International Trade Canada: http://www.infoexport.gc.ca/ieen/DisplayDocument.jsp?did=61388

International Monetary Fund reports on on Latvia, Lithuania, Kazakhstan, the Russian Federation, and Ukraine: http://www.imf.org/external/country

Kari Liuhto, and Jari Jumpponen. "The Internationalization Boom of Russian Corporations – Studies of Russian Banks, Energy and Metal Companies."

Research Report No. 135, Department of Industrial Engineering and Management, Lappeenranta University of Technology, 2002.

Kuchins, Andrew (ed.). *Russia after the Fall*. Washington, D.C.: Carnegie Endowment for International Peace, 2002.

Kuchma, Leonid. *Ukraine is not Russia*. Kyiv, 2004.

Kulikova, Nina. "Russia becomes more attractive to investors." *RIA Novosti* [Moscow], 17 January 2007.

"Latvia economy hits growth peak in 2006." The Associated Press, 9 February 2007.

Lavrov, Vlad. "Foreign companies lining up for Ukrainian uranium," *Kyiv Post*, 1 February, 2007.

Lawrence, Paul R., and Vlachoutsicos, Charalambos Vlachoutsicos, "Joint ventures in Russia: Put the locals in charge." *Harvard Business Review*, January–February 1990: 44–52.

Leitzel, Jim. *Russian Economic Reform*. London/New York: Routledge, 1995.

Macinnis, Laura. "China and Russia named worst for business piracy," *Reuters*, 29 January 2007.

Marinova, Svetla Trifonova, and Marinov, Martin Alexandrov. *Foreign Direct Investment in Central and Eastern Europe*. Aldershot: Ashgate, 2003.

Mayer, Chris. "The Russian bear is back." *MoneyWeek*, 11 February, 2007.

Miller, R.F. "Economic Reform in Ukraine: The Unfinished Agenda." *Slavonic and East European Review*, Volume 80, Number 2, 1 April 2002.

Nicholson, Alex. "Chevron interested in Yukos – Russian official says Bay

Area gas giant could purchase disputed assets," The Associated Press, 10 February, 2007.

Nicholson, Alex. "Putin: Russian Economy Must Diversify," The Associated Press 6 February 2007.

Olcott, Martha Brill. Kazakhstan, Unfulfilled Promise. Washington, D.C.: Carnegie Endowment for International Peace, Brookings Institution Press, 2002.

PriceWaterHouse Coopers – Latvia, Lithuania, Kazakhstan, Russia and Ukraine: http://www.pwc.com

Szymanski, Stefan. "Joint Ventures in Russia: The View from the Russians," *Business Strategy Review,* 9 (3) 1998: 7–14.

Tikhomirov, Vladimir. *The Political Economy of Post-Soviet Russia.* London: Macmillan, 2000.

Timofeyev, Lev. *Russia's Secret Rulers: How the Government and the Criminal Mafia Exercise Their Power.* New York: Alfred A. Knopf, 1992.

"Ukraine exports twice international average." *ForUm,* 25 January, 2007.

United Nations Conference on Trade and Development (UNCTAD) website: http://www.unctad.org

US Department of State: Country Commercial Guides for Latvia, Lithuania, Kazakhstan, Russia and Ukraine. http://www.state.gov

UK Trade and Investment reports on on Latvia, Lithuania, Kazakhstan, the Russian Federation, and Ukraine: https://www.uktradeinvest.gov.uk

Weir, Fred. "Gazprom: rising star of new Kremlin capitalism – The Russian energy giant fuels Moscow's agenda, blurring the line between business and politics," *The Christian Science Monitor,* 23 January 2007.

Weir, Fred. "Kremlin reasserts control of oil, gas – Russia, the world's second-largest oil producer, sees energy as a key foreign policy tool," The Christian Science Monitor 28 January 2005.

Wilson, Andrew. *The Ukrainians: Unexpected Nation.* New Haven: Yale University Press. 2000.

World Bank Reports on Latvia, Lithuania, Kazakhstan, the Russian Federation, and Ukraine: http://web.worldbank.org

DATABASES

Dow Jones
Reuters
Financial Times

Index

Printed and bound by CPI Group (UK) Ltd, Croydon, CR0 4YY